Song

of

Songs

Song
of
Songs

Jeanne Guyon

Whitaker House

All Scripture quotations are from the *King James Version* (KJV) of the Bible.

SONG OF SONGS

ISBN: 0-88368-404-7
Printed in the United States of America
Copyright © 1997 by Whitaker House

Whitaker House
30 Hunt Valley Circle
New Kensington, PA 15068

1 2 3 4 5 6 7 8 9 10 11 12/07 06 05 04 03 02 01 00 99 98 97

Contents

Introduction

Jeanne Guyon (1648–1717) was a Christian contemplative and writer. Being contemplative refers to what is sacredly obscure or secret, something that is remote from human comprehension. It reflects the search for a deeper spiritual life, for fellowship and oneness with the omniscient, omnipotent God who is also our Father.

Jeanne Guyon's commentary on Song of Songs is an allegory of the relationship between Christ and His bride, in which the bride stands for the individual believer rather than the church as a whole. It depicts the believer's journey from spiritual infancy to mature faith and unity with God through Jesus Christ.

The author wrote from the depth of her own spiritual experiences. Growing up in France during the decadent times of Louis the XIV, she was devout at an early age, but was then caught up in the worldliness around her. After an arranged marriage at age fifteen, she became increasingly interested in spiritual things; and, for the rest of her life, she continued to seek God diligently, teach others, and write books on Christian devotion. These books have become Christian classics.

Yet, Jeanne Guyon paid a heavy price for her views and her writings. Throughout her life, she underwent various trials, including persecution and imprisonment for her beliefs. Her commentary on Song of Songs is the very book that was used to sentence her to prison!

Jeanne Guyon wrote this allegorical work for all believers who sincerely want to attain oneness with God. Yet, in many ways, this commentary may also be viewed as a picture of the growth of her own relationship with God, of her devotion to Him in the midst of the losses, illnesses, trials, and persecutions that she endured throughout her life.

Jeanne Guyon used the Vulgate Bible translation. Therefore, minor text alterations have been made to match the King James Version, which is used throughout this edition. Also, many of her lengthy footnotes, which she derived from one of her previous works, *The Justifications,* have been incorporated into the text for easier reading. Her footnotes containing quotations from other authors have been cited and included in the body of the text as well.

For continuity, Scripture references in this edition are cited as Song of Songs, rather than Song of Solomon, as is generally used in the King James Version.

The song of songs, which is Solomon's.
(Song of Songs 1:1)

Chapter 1

The Betrothal

Let him kiss me with the kisses of his mouth. (Song 1:2a)

Song of Songs begins with an announcement of what is to be its conclusion and, as it were, the reward and perfection of the spouse: *the kisses of his mouth.*

This kiss, which the soul desires of her God, is a real, permanent, and lasting possession of her Divine Object. It is the spiritual marriage of the soul with her Maker. To make the nature of this spiritual marriage clear, it is necessary for me to explain that there are two kinds of union with God. One is what I call the union of the powers, that is, the union of the faculties of the soul with God. The other is essential union, and this is what I mean by the spiritual marriage. Either of these two unions may be transitory, and for a few moments only, or permanent and lasting.

It is the vision of consummation, or essential union, that induces the spouse to ask, in the first place, for the kisses of His mouth, though it is the last thing she will receive, and that only after having undergone many a trial and many a toil.

So you may begin to comprehend the process through which the spouse will arrive at essential union, the spiritual progress which is depicted in Song of Songs, a further explanation of the concepts of the union of the powers and essential union is needed. Therefore, let me first describe the union of the powers in more detail. This occurs when God unites the soul to Himself, but very superficially; it is more properly a contact than a union. The soul is nevertheless united to the personal Trinity, according to the different effects that are characteristic of each member. However, it is as if this union is made to the distinct persons of the Trinity, rather than to God in His essential oneness. And it seems to be accomplished by an intermediate action, instead of a direct one. This initial union serves both as a means and an end. The soul rests in the union that it then experiences, without supposing that there is anything beyond it.

This union is accomplished, in order, in all the faculties of the soul (the understanding, the memory, and the will). It is sometimes perceived in one or two of them according to the plans of God, and at other times is seen in all three together. Again, this constitutes the joining of the soul to the Holy Trinity as to distinct persons.

When the union is in the understanding alone, it is a union of pure intellect, and is attributed to the Word as a distinct person.

When the union is in the memory, effected by an absorption of the soul into God and a profound forgetfulness of oneself, it is attributed to the Father as a distinct person.

And when it takes place in the will alone, by a loving joy, without sight or knowledge of anything distinct, it is a union of love, and is attributed to the Holy Spirit as a distinct person. This latter is the most perfect of all, because it comes closer than any other to essential union, and is generally the road by which the soul arrives at it.

All these unions are divine embraces, but they are not the kisses of His mouth. The union of the powers is a union of betrothal; it implies the affection of the heart, caresses, and mutual presents, as is the case with the betrothed, but not the full enjoyment of its Object.

However, essential union, or the kisses of His mouth, is the spiritual marriage, where there is a union of essence with essence and a communication of substance—where God takes the soul for a spouse and unites Himself to it, no longer by persons nor by any act or means, but directly, reducing all into unity and possessing it in His own unity.

Returning to our Scripture text, Song of Songs 1:2*a*, we may therefore understand that essential union, or real and perfect possession, is what is meant by *the kisses of his mouth*. This union is an enjoyment that is neither barren nor unfruitful, since it encompasses nothing less than the communication of the Word of God to the soul.

We must remember that God is all "mouth," as He is all Word, and that the application of the Divine Mouth to the soul is the perfect enjoyment and consummation of the marriage by which the communication of God Himself, and of His Word, is made to the soul.

This is what may be called the apostolic state, in which the soul is not only espoused but fruitful; for God, as mouth, is for some time united to the soul before rendering her fruitful through His own fertility.

There are some who maintain that this union cannot take place until the next life; but

I am confident that it may be attained in this life, with this reservation: that here we possess without seeing, there we will see what we possess.

Consequently, I believe that, while the sight of God will add to our glory in heaven, without which it would be incomplete, it does not, nevertheless, constitute essential blessedness. For, we are happy from the moment we receive the Supreme Good, and can receive and enjoy Him without seeing Him. We enjoy Him here in the night of faith, where we have the pleasure of enjoyment without the satisfaction of sight; there, we will have the clear vision of God in addition to the happiness of possessing Him. But this present blindness hinders neither the true possession nor the genuine enjoyment of the Object, nor the consummation of the divine marriage, any more than it does the real communication of the Word to the soul.

All this is more real than can be expressed, as will be testified by every person who has experienced it. And in the fact that God, in the spiritual marriage, possesses the soul without interruption, we may note the difference between essential union and every other kind.

We can only enjoy being united to another person during certain times, because the other person is external; but the enjoyment of God is permanent and lasting because it is within. Since God is our final goal, the soul can incessantly pour itself into Him as into its Goal and Center, to be mingled and transformed there without ever coming out again—that is, unless it should fall away and be rejected by God. It is the same way with a river, which is composed of water derived from the sea, but is quite distinct from it. When it finds itself away from its source, it endeavors in various ways to reach the ocean; and when it has done so, it loses and mixes itself in it—just as it was mixed with the ocean before it left it—and can no longer be distinguished from it.

It is to be observed further that God, in creating us, made us participants of His being and fit to be reunited with Him. At the same time, He bestowed upon us a tendency toward such a reunion. He has imparted a similar trait to the human body in respect to man in a state of innocence, drawing it from man himself, so that He might give man an inclination to union in marriage that is similar to his inclination to union with his Creator. But as this takes place between whole, physical beings, the union can only be material and very restricted, because it occurs between solid and impenetrable bodies.

This may be illustrated by the attempt to unite two metals of very different qualities by fusing them together. They never can be perfectly united because of their dissimilitude, but the nearer alike the two metals are, the more readily they mix. On the other hand, mix two glasses of water, and the two immediately become so mingled that they are indistinguishable. Therefore, the soul, being perfectly spiritual in its character, is altogether fit to be united, mingled, and transformed in its God.

Consider another example, the union of salt and water. When a lump of rock salt is thrown into water, there is union between the two because they are united on all sides; but when the salt is liquified, dissolved, and vanished, then there is union and admixture.

There may be a union without any intermixture; such is the union of the powers. But the intermingling is the essential union, and this union is absolute. All is in all.

It is only to God that the soul can be united in this way, because such is its nature by creation. This union is what the apostle Paul called being "changed into the same image" (2 Cor. 3:18), and what the Savior called *oneness*. (See John 17:11, 21.)

This oneness, therefore, takes place when the soul loses its own existence to exist only in God. I mean this in a spiritual sense, in the loss of all self-glorification and through a loving and perfect sinking of the soul into Him. I do not mean that essential stripping of intrinsic existence implied in the hypostatic union.[1] What I am referring to may be illustrated by a drop of water falling into a cup of wine. It loses its own appropriate form and character, and is apparently changed into wine; but its being and substance always remain entirely distinct, so that, if it were the will of God, an angel could at any time separate the identical drop. In the same way, the soul can always be separated from God, though with great difficulty.

This, then, is the lofty and intimate union that the spouse in verse two so pressingly demands at the hand of the Bridegroom. She asks it of Him as though she were addressing another, in an impetuous outburst of love, giving vent to her passion without particular thought as to whom she is speaking. *Let him kiss me*, she says, since He can do it, but let it be with the kisses of His mouth; no other union can make me content; that alone can satisfy all my desires, and that is what I demand.

---

[1] Hypostatic union: the union of the divine and human natures in Christ.

Verses 2*b*, 3*a*:

*For thy love is better than wine. Because of
the savour of thy good ointments...*

Your nourishment, O God, with which
You nourish souls in their beginnings, is so
sweet and pleasant that it renders Your children, and even those who still have need of it,
stronger than the stoutest men who are drink-
ers of *wine*. It is so fragrant that, by its
charming perfume, it attracts those souls who
are fortunate enough to perceive it; it is also
like precious *ointments* that heal every interior
wound. Ah! if this is so, even at the outset,
what delights will there not be in the nuptial
kisses, the kisses of His mouth?

Verse 3*b*:

*Thy name is as ointment poured forth,
therefore do the virgins love thee.*

Perceptible grace is signified in this verse
by the *name* of the Bridegroom. It penetrates
the whole soul so powerfully with the sweetness
that God sends to the souls He intends to fill
with His love, that it is truly like an *ointment
poured forth*, which extends and imperceptibly
increases, proportionately, as it is poured out
more and more. It has so excellent an aroma

that the young soul finds herself wholly penetrated by its power and sweetness.

This takes place without force and with so much pleasure that the soul, still young and feeble, allows herself to be carried away by these innocent charms. This is the way God causes Himself to be loved by young hearts, who are not as yet capable of loving except for the sake of the pleasure they experience in loving. It was by a stream of this oil of gladness that the Father anointed the Son above His fellows (Ps. 45:7), who will share His glory with Him.

Verse 4a:

Draw me, we will run after thee.

This young lover pleads with the Bridegroom to draw her by the center of her soul, as if she were not satisfied with the sweetness of the balsam that has been poured forth among her faculties. For she already comprehends, through the grace of the Bridegroom who continually draws her with more and more force, that there is an enjoyment of Himself more noble and more intimate than that which she at present shares. This is what gives rise to her present request.

Draw me, says she, into the most interior chambers of my soul, that my faculties and senses may all run to You by this deeper, though less perceptible, course. *Draw me,* O Divine Lover! and *we will run after thee* by contemplation that causes us to perceive the divine force by which You draw us toward You. In running, we will be guided by a certain scent, perceived by virtue of your attraction. This is the aroma of the ointment You have already poured forth to heal the evil that sin has caused in our faculties, and to purify our senses from the corruption that has entered there. We will even outrun this scent to reach You, the center of our bliss.

This excellent perfume leads to the prayer of contemplation, because the senses, as well as the faculties, all run after its aroma, which causes them to taste with delight that the Lord is good (Ps. 34:8).

Verse 4*b*:

The king hath brought me into his chambers: we will be glad and rejoice in thee, we will remember thy love more than wine: the upright love thee.

The soul has no sooner manifested her desire to pass by all others that she may run to Him, than, to recompense her for a love already somewhat purified, He causes her to enter into

His divine store chambers. This is a greater grace than any she has received up to this point, for she has been in a transient union in the faculties, or powers.

When the heart of a person displays sufficient fidelity to be willing to dispense with all the gifts of God that it may reach God Himself, He takes pleasure in showering upon it a profusion of the very gifts it did not seek; but He removes them with indignation from those who prefer them to seeking Him alone.

It was a knowledge of this that caused the royal prophet to urge all men to "seek the LORD, and his strength: seek his face evermore" (Ps. 105:4), as though he were saying: Do not stop at the graces or gifts of God, which are only as the rays that issue from His face, but which are not Himself. Mount up to His very throne and seek Him there. "Seek his face evermore" until you are so blessed as to find it.

Then, says the spouse, transported with joy at the inexpressible secret revealed to her, then, when we are in You, O God, *we will be glad and rejoice in thee, we will remember thy love more than wine.* That is, the remembrance of having preferred the Bridegroom over everything else will be the height of her joy and pleasure. She has already chosen the sweetness of His milk over the wine of the pleasures of this world.

That is why she says, We will remember your
love more than wine. Here she chooses God in
preference to His spiritual consolations and the
transports of grace, which she experienced
while drawing nourishment from Him.

She adds, *The upright love thee*, to signify
that true uprightness, which leads the soul to
dispense with all the pleasures of earth and the
enjoyments of heaven, to be lost in God, is
what constitutes pure and perfect love. Truly,
O my God, none but those who live uprightly
can love You as You deserve to be loved!

Verse 5:

*I am black, but comely, O ye daughters of
Jerusalem, as the tents of Kedar, as the
curtains of Solomon.*

As the greatest graces of God tend always
to produce in us a deeper knowledge of what
we are, and as they would not come from Him
if they did not give, in their degree, a certain
taste of the misery of created beings, so it is
with this soul. Scarcely has she emerged from
the store chambers of the King before she discovers that she is *black*.

We say to her, What is this blackness, O
you incomparable maiden? Tell us, we beg you.

I am black, she answers, because I perceive, by the light of my Divine Sun, hosts of defects, of which I was never aware until now; I am black, because I am not yet cleansed of self. But, nevertheless, I am as beautiful as the *tents of Kedar.*[2] For, this knowledge of what I am, which comes through personal experience, is extremely pleasing to my Bridegroom, and induces Him to visit me as a place of rest. I am beautiful because, having no voluntary stain, my Spouse renders me fair with His own beauty. The blacker I am in my own eyes, the fairer I am in His. I am as beautiful, too, *as the curtains of Solomon.* The curtains of the Divine Solomon are the holy humanity that conceals the Word of God made flesh. I am as beautiful as His curtains, for He has made me a partaker of His beauty in this way: that as the holy humanity concealed the Divinity, so my apparent blackness hides the greatness of God's workings in my soul.

She adds, I am black also from the crosses and persecutions that attack me from outside;

---

[2] Tents of Kedar: Kedar apparently refers to a tribe that was named after Kedar, Abraham's grandson through Ishmael. The people were nomads in the northern part of the Arabian Desert, living in tents and raising sheep, goats, and camels.

but I am as attractive as the curtains of Solomon, because blackness and the Cross make me like Him. I am black because outward weaknesses (not sins) appear in me, but I am beautiful, because my intention is pure within.

Verse 6:

Look not upon me, because I am black, because the sun hath looked upon me: my mother's children were angry with me; they made me the keeper of the vineyards; but mine own vineyard have I not kept.

Why is it that the betrothed asks them not to look upon her in her blackness? She asks this because as she is now entering into the state of faith, and is being robbed of perceptible grace, she is losing by degrees the sweet vigor that led her so easily to the practice of virtue, and made her externally so beautiful.

When the soul still felt the full power of the divine grace upon her, her imperfections appeared to be destroyed; but, as the work of purification goes on, the virtues sink deep into the soul, disappearing from the surface and leaving the natural defects in conspicuous prominence.

The effects of winter upon plant life seem to me to present a living and truthful image of this operation of God. As the season of cold and storms approaches, the trees gradually lose their leaves, their vivid green is soon changed into a funeral brown, and they fall and die. The trees now look stripped and desolate; the loss of their summer garments brings to light all the irregularities and defects in their surfaces, which had previously been hidden from view. It is not that they have contracted any new deformity; not at all, everything was there before but was hidden by their abundant foliage. Therefore, a person in the time of his purification appears stripped of his virtues; but, as the tree, in the preservation of its sap, retains that which produces its leaves, so the soul is not deprived of the essence of virtue, nor of any secure advantage, but only of a certain external facility in the display of its possessions. The person who is plundered and naked in this way appears in his own eyes, and in those of others, to have all the defects of nature that were previously concealed by the foliage of perceptible grace.

During the entire winter the trees appear dead; they are not so in reality, but, on the contrary, are submitting to a process that preserves and strengthens them. For what is the effect of winter? It contracts their exteriors, so that the sap is not uselessly expended, and it concentrates their strength on the root, so that new roots are pushed out and old ones are strengthened and nourished and forced deeper into the soil. We may say then, that however dead the tree may appear in its nonessential qualities (if we may be allowed to apply this expression to its leaves), it was never more alive in its essentials. And it is expressly during winter that the source and principle of its life are more firmly established. During the other seasons, it employs the whole force of its sap in adorning and beautifying itself at the expense of its roots.

It is the same way in the economy of grace. God takes away that which is "nonessential" in virtue, that He may strengthen the principle of the virtues. The virtues are still practiced by the soul, though in an exceedingly hidden way; and in humility, pure love, absolute abandonment, denial of self, and the other virtues, the soul makes solid progress. It is through this process that the operation of God seems to tarnish the soul on the exterior; in actuality, it indicates no new defects in the soul, but only an uncovering of the old ones so that, by being openly exposed, they may be better healed.

Therefore, the spouse, not being able any longer to perform her previous acts because God requires something else of her, seems to have fallen back into a state of nature. Yet it only appears this way to those who are not enlightened, and it is for this reason that she exclaims, I implore you, my friends and companions who have not yet arrived at so interior a point, you who are still in the first experiences of the spiritual life, do not judge me because I am dark-colored externally, nor because of my outward defects, real or apparent. For they do not occur from a lack of love and courage, as is the case with souls when they are first starting out, but because my Divine Sun *hath looked upon me* with His constant, burning beams, and has changed my color. He has taken away my natural complexion, that I might have only the kind of complexion that His fiery fervor would give me. It is the force of love, she says, and not its departure, that dries up and tans my skin.

Consider how fire blackens wood before consuming it. It is the approach of the fire, and not its removal, that blackens the wood. Wood may also be discolored by moisture; but it is then far less fit to be burned, and may even be made so wet that it will not burn at all. Such is the blackness of those who depart from You, O God, and go whoring from You (Ps. 73:27). They will all perish, but this is not the case with our spouse. She is rendered dark complected by an overflow of love; God intends to perfect her in Himself by cleansing her of everything opposed to His own purity.

The spouse continues speaking to her friends and companions. This blackness, she says, is an advance, not a relapse; but it is not a progress for you to imitate at your tender age, for the blackness that you would give yourselves would be a defect. To be right, it must only proceed from the Sun of Righteousness, who, for His own glory and the highest good of the soul, burns up and destroys that dazzling outward complexion that was a source of blindness to the soul—though a cause of great admiration to those around, to the great injury of the Bridegroom's glory.

My mother's children, seeing me black, sought to compel me to resume my active life and to direct my attention to the exterior, instead of devoting myself to the destruction of my interior passions. They strove against me for a long while, and, in the end, not being able to resist them, I yielded to their desires. But, in attending to these outward and foreign things, *mine own vineyard have I not kept,* which is my interior, where my God dwells. To that vineyard belongs my whole care, and it is the only vineyard I ought to keep. Moreover, since I have not kept my own vineyard, since I have been inattentive to the voice of my God, I have been still less faithful in guarding those of others.

This is the persecution that souls are ordinarily subjected to, once it is perceived that their constant introversion causes them to neglect some external thing. The soul is entirely turned inward and, therefore, is not able to apply herself to the correction of certain trifling defects that the Bridegroom will Himself remedy in due time.

Verse 7:

Tell me, O thou whom my soul loveth, where thou feedest, where thou makest thy flock to rest at noon: for why should I be as one that turneth aside by the flocks of thy companions?

O thou whom my soul loveth! exclaims this poor betrothed one, who has been obliged to leave the sweet occupation within, to become engaged in external matters of the lowest description; O You whom I love all the more, the more I find my love thwarted; ah, show me where You feed your flocks, and with what food You satisfy the souls who are so blessed as to be under your care! We know that when You were upon the earth, Your meat and drink were to do the will of Your Father (see John

4:34); and now Your meat is that Your friends
do Your will. You still feed Your followers with
Yourself, revealing to them Your infinite perfections so that they may love You more fer-
vently. And the more You are revealed, the
more they seek to know, that they always may
be able to love You more and more.

Tell me also, she pursues, where You repose *at noon*. By this analogy, she intends to
convey the vehemence of pure love, desiring to
learn, from its Author and Master, of what it
consists. She does this for fear that she may
perhaps wander into some human path, though
under the semblance of spirituality. She is also
afraid that she may be misled and may minister
to self-love at the very moment that she is persuaded that she has no other motivation except
pure love and the glory of God alone.

She is right to fear a mistake that involves
such important consequences, and which is too
common among the flocks of the church. This
mistake occurs whenever people are guided by
spiritual advisers whom Jesus Christ has truly
rendered His companions, associating them
with Himself in the teaching of souls, but who,
not being dead to themselves nor crucified to
the world with Him, do not teach their pupils
to deny themselves and to be crucified and
dead in everything, in order to live to God

alone, that Christ may live in them. Therefore, it happens that, since both teachers and pupils are living extremely carnal and self-gratifying lives, their paths are also exceedingly human. Consequently, they are liable to turn aside here and there, frequently changing their loyalties and their guides, without ever arriving at anything solid.

This wandering arises from their failure to consult with care the maxims and example of Jesus Christ, and to apply to Him by prayer to obtain from Him what He alone can grant us. It is for this reason that this beloved soul, being well instructed, implores with so much earnestness the knowledge of His Word, with which He feeds souls, as well as faithfulness to follow His example. For she knows that these alone, with the help of grace, can prevent her from going astray.

We are too often stopped by created methods, however religious. God alone can teach us to do His will, for He alone is our God. (See Psalm 143:10.) Consider this example from John of the Cross:

A father has caused various dishes to be placed upon the table, some far more delicious than others. One of the children has taken a fancy to the dish that stands nearest him, though it is far from the best, and requests to be helped from it because of his liking for it. The father perceives that if he were to give him a far better one he would reject it, his mind being set upon that which he sees before him; and so, lest he should remain hungry and discouraged, he reluctantly grants him his request. Thus God granted the prayer of the Israelites for a king; it was not what He would have chosen for them, nor what they needed, but it was what their hearts were set upon having.[3]

The spouse also asks the Word to conduct her to His Father, since He is the Way that leads there. As the bosom of the Father is the place where He rests in the culmination of His glory, and in the full light of eternity, she desires to be lost in God with Jesus His Son, to be hidden there and to rest there forever. And though she does not say this explicitly, she leads us to understand it distinctly enough by what she says afterwards: *Why should I be as one that turneth aside*, as I have done? In the bosom of the Father I will be perfectly secure;

---

[3] *Ascent of Mount Carmel*, Book ii., ch. 21. John of the Cross (1542–1591) was a Spanish-born Christian mystic and poet who was the author of several works including *The Dark Night of the Soul*.

I will never again be deceived; and what is far better, I will sin no more.

Verse 8:

If thou know not, O thou fairest among women, go thy way forth by the footsteps of the flock, and feed thy kids beside the shepherds' tents.

In this verse, the Bridegroom replies to His bride; and to prepare her for the grace that He desires to bestow, as well as to instruct her in the use of what she has already received, He gives her a most important direction: *If thou know not*, He says, *go thy way forth*. He means that she cannot know the Divine Object of her love, however passionately she may desire it, unless she first knows herself, for acknowledging the nothingness of mankind enables us to conceptualize the "all" of God. But as the spiritual insight necessary for discovering man's abyss of nothingness exists only in the all of God, He directs her to go forth. From where? From herself. How? By applying abandonment and faithfulness to everything, permitting herself no natural satisfaction and no life in self or any other person.

Let us note here that our spouse, far from falling into open sin, does not even indulge herself in innocent recreations. A soul who has enjoyed God in an unspeakable degree, has acquired too refined a taste to be pleased any longer with earthly things. Those who leave Him, and permit themselves to be guilty of offenses against Him, are those who sought Him only for His delights, not for Himself; when He takes these delights away, such people seek their pleasure elsewhere. But God never abandons a soul who seeks Him for Himself alone, who fears, rather than desires, His favors, and who loves the Cross without fearing it.

The souls who relapse and fall away do so because, in their first deprivation, they seek a compensation, in the pleasures of the senses—which they at first consider innocent—for the suffering inflicted by God. Therefore, I have always strenuously insisted, in everything that He has permitted me to write, that the soul must allow itself to be consumed without seeking consolation, and to die without helping itself to a single breath.

This matter seems to me one of great consequence. For almost every soul, upon arriving at this point, either turns back, seeking again its former activity in order to recover the enjoyment it has lost, or, what is far worse, follows its sensual inclinations. And as the love it had for God was impure, sensual, and entirely selfish, when it no longer feels it, it indulges its senses in the delights of fallen man. As these people loved God solely for the gratification it gave them, as Saint Francis de Sales[4] testifies of them, and not for Himself, the moment their pleasure ceases, they turn to those pleasures that are unlawful. And, as their taste has been refined by their participation in spiritual enjoyments, they cannot now be satisfied without an infinity of pleasure—nor are they then satisfied—but seek to stifle their consciences and their constant remorse by a more unbridled license. Had they loved God with a pure affection, He never would have allowed them to fall in this way.

Let me also add here that, in the beginning, when the soul is immersed in delights and heavenly consolations, it appears strong, but is in fact so exceedingly weak, that the least incidents distract it and cause it to commit a thousand faults. After the first cleansing, or trial, called the "night of the senses" by John of the Cross, the soul is no longer subject to these frailties, so that, regarding its dealings with every external thing in the order of God, it can walk about without being sullied, as formerly, by a thousand vain complacencies

---

[4] Saint Francis de Sales (1567–1622): Bishop of Geneva and writer.

and self-seekings. I refer to external things in the order of God and according to His will, for it would be a very different matter if the soul were to amuse and divert itself. A soul who has reached this state of cleansing could not divert itself without great pain, and without an infidelity so much the more horrible since the soul had the greater power to avoid it.

This is truly the most dangerous period of the whole spiritual life. If, upon the cessation of interior support, the soul turns to external sources of pleasure, even though it finds it difficult at first, that way eventually grows more and more easy. It is a way of destruction for many a spiritual pilgrim, and I have, therefore, in all my writings, constantly pointed it out.

I am speaking of the beginning of the night of the senses, and not when it has fully set in, for then there is scarcely anything to fear. And so, after total "death," the soul becomes so confirmed in God that it can find nothing satisfying in human things, nor can it fall, short of becoming like Lucifer.

To leave God after reaching this state would render a soul the most miserable in the universe. For, as it has tasted the joy unspeakable of the divine union, it cannot with its utmost exertion derive any pleasure from exterior sources. The now distant pleasures of the senses would seem so insipid in comparison with celestial delights, that they would only redouble the soul's torture. Such a soul must be, as it were, in hell. Having received in heaven a divine power, and being now cast out, it must either return to God, a very difficult thing, or must become worse than Satan himself. Such a person, of whom it is difficult to find one, would, I think, become the most abandoned of men, and his depravity would be measured by the extent to which he had experienced the divine favor.

We scarcely ever find, then, a soul who has fallen in this way. However, among those who are just entering into the night of the senses, and who are not yet dead to self, nor established in God, we may see many who, no longer experiencing the delights that they had sought rather than God, turn to human things for the enjoyment that they no longer find in Him. But the pleasures they derive from this are so blunted that they must run to every excess to produce any emotion. It is a miracle when souls in this condition are converted and return to God. For, as they have tasted the good things of God, and have abandoned Him, every motive that can be brought to bear upon them, to bring them back, is already familiar to them; they know it all and it affects them no longer. This, it seems to me, is the meaning of what is declared in the Word:

> *For it is impossible for those who were once enlightened, and have tasted of the heavenly gift, and were made partakers of the Holy Ghost, and have tasted the good word of God, and the powers of the world to come, if they shall fall away, to renew them again unto repentance.* (Heb. 6:4–6)

However, if falling away is difficult for souls in this stage, it is far more so, I might rather say almost impossible, for those in the subsequent ones; for they become, as it were, settled in a fixed state. So great is the difficulty of falling from this state, that it requires the pride of the Devil himself and a maliciousness of purpose of which the soul, at this point, is far from capable. Still, it is, of course, possible, and I suppose there are some who, like the rebel angels, have been thrust headlong down from heaven into hell. (See Isaiah 14:12–15; Luke 10:18.) Yet, after such a fall, the difficulty of returning to God is greatly increased. It seems to me almost impossible, not from any opposition on the part of God, who always furnishes everyone with all essential means of salvation, but because of the wickedness in which such a soul is strengthening and confirming itself. If I may speak after the manner of men, the loss of such a soul is more painful to God than that of a million others, and His former love for them is now the measure of His wrath.

But, returning to the spouse, where is she to go forth? She is to enter into God by an absolute self-abandonment, where she will find that "by him all things consist" (Col. 1:17). He is All and is in all. Therefore, she herself, along with every other person, is merely nothingness.

Now, nothingness deserves no esteem, because it has no good in it; neither does it merit love, for it is nothing. It is only worthy, on the contrary, of contempt and hatred because of its self-conceit and self-centeredness, which are entirely opposed to God, and which have been implanted in it by sin. If a person, then, aspires to divine union, he must be well persuaded of the all of God and his own nothingness. He must go forth from himself, feeling nothing but contempt and hatred for himself, that he may reserve all his esteem and love for God; and in this way, he may attain to union.

This going forth from self by a perpetual abandonment of every selfish interest, is the interior work that the heavenly Bridegroom prescribes for those who are sighing after the kisses of His mouth. He signifies it to this soul by the single expression, *go thy way forth*, which is sufficient to guide her inward course.

Regarding her outward life, it is His will that she should neglect no part of her duty in the station in which He has placed her, a directive that implies infinitely more than the most minute detail could do. And while she must follow the attraction of the Holy Spirit in all liberty regarding her inward life, He would also have her conform to the external usages of religion and be obedient to those in authority in her exterior life. This is what He expresses with the words: *go thy way forth by the footsteps of the flock,* that is to say, in the ordinary, common way, externally; and, *feed thy kids,* that is, the senses, *beside the shepherds' tents.*

Verse 9:

I have compared thee, O my love, to a company of horses in Pharaoh's chariots.

The Bridegroom, knowing perfectly well that all the commendations that He lavishes on His beloved, far from rendering her vain, only further her death to self, praises her in magnificent strains, that her love may be fed. *I have compared thee*, He says, *to a company of horses*. That is, I desire of you a course so swift and sure in Me that I can only compare your single soul to a whole company running toward Me with extreme rapidity. I have compared you to My angels, and I will for you the same bliss that they enjoy: always to behold My face. (See Matthew 18:10.)

He continues, Still, in order to better conceal such great things while you are upon the earth, I have made you externally as *Pharaoh's chariots*. Those who see you running so swiftly and, as it were, disorderly, will believe that you are in search of the pleasures, the vanities, and the numerous false gods of Egypt, or that you are busy in self-seeking, because of your eager haste. But you are running toward Me, and your race will end in Me alone; and nothing will prevent your safe arrival because of the strength and fidelity with which I have supplied you.

Verse 10:

Thy cheeks are comely with rows of jewels,[5]
thy neck with chains of gold.

The *cheeks* signify both the interior and exterior; they are as beautiful as a turtle dove's. The dove is said to have this attribute, that when one of a pair dies, the other forever after

---

[5] In the Vulgate, "with rows of jewels" was translated, "as a turtle dove's," and that is the meaning Jeanne Guyon uses here.

remains single, without seeking another mate. So the soul, separated from her God, can take no pleasure in any other person, either internally or externally. Internally, she is reduced to a solitude so much the more complete, in that, not finding the Bridegroom, she cannot be occupied with anything else. Externally, everything is dead, so far as she is concerned; it is this very separation of the soul from every person and from everything that is not God that constitutes her beauty in the eyes of the Well Beloved.

Her *neck* represents pure love, which is the greatest support left to her. But though she appears in a state of the greatest nakedness, she is still enriched by the practice of numberless virtues, which, like jewels of great price, serve as an adornment. But without this adornment, love alone would render her perfectly beautiful, just as the neck of the bride, though stripped of jewels, is not deprived of beauty.

Verse 11:

We will make thee borders of gold with studs of silver.

Although you are already very beautiful in your nakedness, the evidence of a pure heart and unfeigned love, we will still give you something further to set off your beauty: precious ornaments. These will represent your perfect submission to the will of the King of Glory.

They will be *of gold,* to signify that, acting only from an exceedingly purified love, you have only a single and pure regard for the good pleasure and glory of God in everything you do or suffer for Him. Nevertheless, they will be inlaid with *silver,* because, however simple and pure love may be in itself, it must be made manifest externally, in the practice of good works and the most excellent virtues.

It is to be noted that the Divine Master takes special care in many passages to instruct His beloved pupil regarding the supreme purity He requires in the love of the spouse, and in her faithfulness to neglect nothing in the service of the Well Beloved, or in helping her neighbor.

Verse 12:

While the king sitteth at his table, my spikenard sendeth forth the smell thereof.

The spouse is not yet so unclothed but that she receives, from time to time, visits from her Well Beloved. But why do I call them visits? They are rather manifestations of Himself, experiences of His deep and central presence.

The Holy Bridegroom is always in the center of the soul who is faithful to Him; but He often dwells there in such a hidden way that she is almost always ignorant of her happiness, except at certain times when He is pleased to reveal Himself to the loving soul, who then perceives Him to be deeply and intimately present. Such is His conduct toward this, the purest of His followers, as is testified by her words: *While the king*, He who reigns over and guides me as a sovereign, *sitteth at his table, my spikenard,* that is, my fragrant ointment, my faithfulness, *sendeth forth the smell thereof* so sweetly and pleasantly that He is obliged to reveal Himself to me. Now I recognize that He is reposing within me as on His royal couch, of which earlier I was ignorant; for although He was there, I did not know it.

Verse 13:

A bundle of myrrh is my wellbeloved unto me; he shall lie all night betwixt my breasts.

When the bride, or rather the betrothed (for she is not yet a bride), has found her Bridegroom, she is so transported with joy, that she is eager to be instantly united to Him. But the union of perpetual enjoyment has not yet arrived. He is mine, she says; I cannot doubt that He gives Himself to me this moment, since I perceive it, but He is to me, as it were, *a bundle of myrrh*. He is not yet a Bridegroom whom I may embrace in the nuptial bed, but a bundle of crosses, pains, and mortifications; a bloody husband (see Exodus 4:25) and crucified lover, who desires to test my faithfulness by making me a partaker of a good share of His sufferings. For this is the portion given to the soul at this period.

As an evidence, however, of the progress of this already heroic soul, note that she does not say that her Well Beloved will give her the bundle of the Cross, but that He Himself is that bundle; for, she says, All my crosses will be those of my Well Beloved.

This bundle will be *betwixt my breasts* as an evidence that He will be a Bridegroom of bitterness externally as well as within. External crosses are a small matter, if unaccompanied by those that are internal, and the inward are rendered much more painful by the simultaneous presence of the outward. But though the soul perceives nothing but the Cross on every side, it is nevertheless her Well Beloved in the shape of the Cross; and He is never more present to her than in those seasons of bitterness, during which He dwells in the midst of her heart.

Verse 14:

My beloved is unto me as a cluster of camphire in the vineyards of Engedi.

My beloved, continues the betrothed, is *as a cluster of camphire*[6] to me. She only partially expresses herself. It is as though she were saying: He is only near to me, for I do not have the blessedness of that intimate union by which He would dwell wholly in me, and I in Him. He is nevertheless near to me, but as a cluster of camphire, since it is He alone who gives an aroma and value to everything that is done by those who love Him. This cluster grows *in the vineyards of Engedi,* which are very beautiful, and the grapes of which are excellent.[7] She compares her Well Beloved to the pleasant fragrance and excellent qualities of balsam, and to the delight and strength of wine. Through these images, she expresses that those who have learned, from the interior enjoyment of God, to

---

[6] Camphire: henna, a small, thorny shrub with beautiful white flowers that hang in clusters and are very fragrant.

[7] Engedi: A major oasis along the west coast of the Dead Sea, 35 miles southeast of Jerusalem. It was known for its rich vegetation, owing to its warm springs.

put their pleasure in Him, can no longer find delight in anything else, and that we no sooner seek any other source of satisfaction than we lose that which is divine.

Verse 15:

Behold, thou art fair, my love; behold, thou art fair; thou hast doves' eyes.

The Well Beloved, seeing the readiness of the spouse to be crucified and instructed by Him, is charmed with the luster of the beauty He has bestowed upon her. He caresses and praises her, calling her His fair one and His well beloved. *Behold, thou art fair, my love,* He says; *behold, thou art fair!*

Sweet words! He refers to a double beauty, one external, the other internal; but, He desires that she should perceive it, as though He were saying, See, you are fair already in the depths, though you are not yet perfected. Know, too, that in a little while you will be perfectly beautiful on the outside, when I have finished you and drawn you out of your weaknesses.

These praises are accompanied by the promise of a more exquisite beauty, in the hope of which the soul will take courage while her humility is cultivated as she reflects on her imperfections. But why does He say that in a little while she will be crowned with a double beauty? It is because she already has *doves' eyes*. That is, she is simple within, not turning aside from the sight of her God. And she is also simple on the outside, in all her words and actions, which are totally without guile.

This dove-like simplicity is the surest mark of the advancement of the soul. For, no longer making use of indirect means or methods, she is led by the Spirit of God. The spouse understood from the beginning the necessity of simplicity, and the perfect nature of uprightness, when she said, *The virgins*, meaning the upright, *love thee* (Song 1:3). In this she recognized that the perfection of love is in its simplicity and uprightness.

Verse 16:

Behold, thou art fair, my beloved, yea, pleasant: also our bed is green.

The loving soul, seeing that her Bridegroom has praised her for her double beauty, and unwilling to appropriate anything to herself, says in return, *Behold, thou art fair, my beloved, yea, pleasant*. She returns to Him all the praise she has received from Him, and adds more on her own part. Since nothing belongs to us—no praise, no glory, and no pleasure—everything must be referred to Him who is the Author and Center of every good. The loving soul teaches us this important point of practice throughout. She always gives glory to the Lord for everything He has bestowed upon her. If I am beautiful, she says to Him, it is with Your own beauty; it is You who are beautiful in me with this double beauty, which You praise in me.

Our bed, she adds, that inner retreat in which You dwell in me, and which I call ours, so that You may be induced to come there and give me the nuptial kiss that I first asked of You, and which is my final consummation—our bed is ready and *green* with a thousand virtues.

Verse 17:

The beams of our house are cedar, and our rafters of fir.

The Bridegroom, hidden in the ground and center of the soul (as has been said), takes pleasure in sending, from the sanctuary in which He dwells, rivers of His perceivable graces. These produce, in the exterior of the spouse, an abundance of different virtues that are like flowers. Finding herself adorned with these, she is so surprised and charmed, or perhaps has so little experience, that she believes her inward edifice is nearly completed.

The roof is on, she says; *the beams* (which are the practice of exterior virtues) *are cedar*; I think that I perceive their agreeable scent and that I can practice them with as much strength as ease. The ordering of the senses appears to me to be as perfectly accomplished as the setting in order of the beautiful *rafters of fir*.

But, O spouse! this only appears so to you because your bed is adorned with flowers, and because the sweet, agreeable, and pleasant state that you experience within makes you believe that you have gained everything without. But remember, your rafters are of fir, which is a tree of death,[8] and all this beauty and adornment are but the preparation for a sacrifice.

---

[8] Branches of the evergreen cypress are used as an emblem of mourning; they were used at funerals in ancient times.

Chapter 2

Seeking His Countenance

I am the rose of Sharon, and the lily of the valleys. (Song 2:1)

*T*his, O my God, is a gentle reproach to Your spouse for desiring so soon to repose upon a flowery couch, before having rested with You upon the painful bed of the Cross. *I am the rose of Sharon*, the Bridegroom says, a flower you will not find in the repose of the couch, but which must be culled in the field of combat, labor, and suffering. *I am the lily of the valleys*, which only grows in souls who have died to themselves. If, then, you want Me to uproot you from earth, that I may take root in you, you must be in the most extreme annihilation. If you want to find Me, you must engage in combat and endure hardship.

Verse 2:

As the lily among thorns, so is my love among the daughters.

By these words, the Bridegroom indicates the progress of His beloved, since she is like a *lily,* very pure and pleasant, and of a sweet scent before Him. She is in contrast to the other *daughters,* who, instead of being obedient and pliable and allowing themselves to be led by His Spirit, are like a thicket of *thorns* that is impenetrable and wounds those who attempt to approach it. These are souls who are self-possessed and immersed in their own wills, who refuse to be guided toward God. And it is a cause of suffering to a soul who is abandoned to God when she is placed among people like this, for they do all that lies in their power to draw her from the right path. Yet the lily perfectly preserves both its purity and its perfume, even when surrounded by thorns. In the same way, these souls who are abandoned to the Bridegroom are preserved by Him in the midst of the opposition they experience from those who prefer to be their own guides and to dwell in their own numerous works, those who have no obedience in following the movement of grace.

Verse 3:

As the apple tree among the trees of the wood, so is my beloved among the sons. I sat down under his shadow with great delight, and his fruit was sweet to my taste.

How much simplicity there is in this comparison! The beloved, seeing herself persecuted by spiritual persons who do not understand her experience, addresses herself to them and to her Well Beloved at the same time. *As the apple tree among the trees of the wood, so is my beloved among the sons*, that is, among those most pleasing in the sight of God, whether saints in heaven or the righteous upon the earth. Do not be surprised then, she says, if I sit down *under his shadow*, and remain at rest under His protection. I am only under the shadow of the wings of Him by whom I have greatly desired to be possessed. And although I have not yet arrived at so desirable an attainment, I can say that *his fruit*, that is, crosses, pain, and abasement, is *sweet to my taste*. It is not sweet to the taste of the flesh, for the inferior part finds it bitter and ill-flavored. However, it is sweet to the mouth of the heart, after it is once swallowed. And for me, whose taste is that of my Well Beloved, it is more to be desired than all other delights.

Verse 4:

He brought me to the banqueting house,
and his banner over me was love.

The beloved of the King, as the result of
her delightful meetings with Him, appears to
her companions to be intoxicated and beside
herself. And truly she is in this state, for,
having tasted of the finest wine of the Bridegroom at His banquet, she could not help being
seized with the most extreme devotion. Being
quite sensible of it herself, she begs her companions not to be amazed at seeing her in so
extraordinary a condition.

My intoxication, she says, is excusable, for
my King has *brought me to the banqueting
house, and his banner over me* [is] *love*. The
first time He made me a partaker of such singular grace I was so feeble that I would rather
have preferred the sweetness of the divine
breasts to the strength of this excellent wine.
Therefore, He was content to show me its effects, allowing me to drink only a little of it.
But now that experience and His grace have
rendered me wiser and stronger, I can no
longer drink only a little. I have drunk so
abundantly of His strong and pure wine, that
His banner over me is love.

What manner of love does God ordain? O Love! O God of charity! You alone can reveal it!

He causes this soul, who, by a movement of love, desired for herself every possible good in reference to God, to forget herself wholly so that she may only think upon her Well Beloved. She becomes divested of every selfish interest in her own salvation, perfection, joy, or consolation, so that she may only think of the interests of God. She no longer thinks of enjoying His embrace, but of suffering for Him. She no longer asks anything for herself, but only that He may be glorified. She enters fully into the purposes of the Divine Righteousness, consenting with all her heart to everything He decrees in her and with respect to her, whether for time or eternity. She can love nothing in herself or in any other person, except in and for God—not in and for self—however important and necessary it may appear.

Such is the order of love that God ordains in this soul. Her love has become perfectly chaste. All others are nothing to her; she wills them only for her God, and none of them for herself. Ah! what strength does this well-ordered love impart for the terrible states that are to follow! However, this strength can only be known and enjoyed by those who have experienced it. The others have not yet tasted of the Bridegroom's wine.

Verse 5:

Stay me with flagons, comfort me with apples: for I am sick of love.

The Bridegroom has no sooner so ordered love in the soul, than He bestows upon her special grace to prepare her for the sufferings that are to follow. He gives her His transitory union in her center, which from there expands into the senses and faculties. And as she is not yet very strong, there is, as it were, an absorption or suspension of the senses that forces her to cry out, *Stay me with flagons,*[1] help me with some little external practices—or, *comfort me with apples*, some of the fruits of the exercise of love—so that I will not die under these powerful charms. For, I perceive that *I am sick of love*.

Poor child! What are you saying? Why do you talk of being comforted by exterior consolations—mere trifles? You do not know what you ask; forgive my plainness. If you faint under this trial, you only fall into the arms of your

---

[1] Flagon: A large vessel with a narrow mouth, used for holding and transporting liquor, such as wine.

Loved One! And happy would you be to die there! But you are not yet prepared for this.

Verse 6:

His left hand is under my head, and his right hand doth embrace me.

She begins to understand the mystery, and, repenting of the foreign support she had sought, she says, *His left hand is under my head.* He bears me up with exceptional care, since He has honored me with union with Himself in the powers of my soul. What business do I have then with exterior consolations, that is, with things that are material and human, since He favors me with those that are divine? He is even going on to do more for me, uniting me to Himself in essence. And I will then be fruitful and produce for my Bridegroom fruits incomparably more beautiful than those I desired. For, He will *embrace me* with His *right hand*, which is His omnipotence accompanied by His love, with the chaste embraces that produce in the soul the perfect enjoyment of Him, which is only another name for essential union.

It is true that, at first, this embrace of the right hand is the betrothal of the soul, but not its marriage. He will embrace me, she says; He will first bind me to Himself by the tie of betrothal, by which I have the hope of a future marriage, when He will so embrace me and so bind me to Himself that I will fear no subsequent defection.

For the distinguishing characteristic of essential union is that it strengthens the soul so fully that it no longer allows those fears and weaknesses that beset souls who are just starting out—those who, grace being still feeble in them, experience relapses and falls. In this strengthened state, the soul is confirmed in love, since it then dwells in God; and the one who dwells in love, dwells in God, for God is love. (See 1 John 4:16.)

Verse 7:

I charge you, O ye daughters of Jerusalem,
by the roes, and by the hinds of the field,
that ye stir not up, nor awake my love, till
[she] *please.*

The soul is in a mystic slumber in this embrace of betrothal, in which she enjoys a sacred rest she has never before experienced. In her previous intervals of repose, she had indeed rested under His shadow by her confidence in Him, but she had never slept upon His bosom nor in His arms.

It is strange how eager people are, even those who are spiritual, to awaken the soul from this gentle slumber. Those who are beginning to serve God are commonly persecuted by the unregenerate, because their withdrawal is a public condemnation of the unlawfulness that reigns in the world. However, the more these new believers are condemned by the unregenerate, the more they are esteemed by people of righteousness.

Not so, however, with those who devote themselves to the interior life; not only do they suffer persecution at the hands of a godless world and from people who live regular lives, but far more severely from pious and spiritually minded persons who are not devoted to the interior life. These latter do it as a matter of duty, not being able to recognize any other way as right but that in which they themselves are walking.

But the most violent assaults come from so-called saints and false devotees, whose foul characters, wickedness, and hypocrisies are detected by those who are as devoted to God as they are enlightened by His truth. This gives rise to an opposition between the false saints and those who are truly spiritual, like that between the devils and the angels.

The *daughters of Jerusalem* in this verse are loving and meddlesome souls who are anxious to wake her, though under the most specious pretexts, but she is so soundly asleep that she cannot be roused. Then the Bridegroom speaks for her, and, clasping her in His arms, charges them by what they esteem most highly—the practice of the most ardent and active virtues—not to awaken His love, nor to disturb her rest, for she is more pleasing to Him in this rest than she would be in all her external activity. Wake her not, He says, either directly or indirectly, nor use any far-fetched clever schemes to accomplish your purpose; let her rest until she please, for she will please, whenever I please.

Verse 8:

The voice of my beloved! behold, he cometh leaping upon the mountains, skipping upon the hills.

The soul, asleep to everything else, is only the more attentive to the voice of her Well Beloved; she hears and recognizes it at once.

The voice of my beloved! she exclaims; I know it, I hear it, and its effects upon me remove all my doubts.

But what are you saying, O beloved one? You are perhaps dreaming from love; though you are asleep in the arms of your Bridegroom, you see Him *leaping upon the mountains, skipping upon the hills!* How then can this be?

The Bridegroom embraces His beloved and dwells in her. He surrounds her on the outside and penetrates her within. She feels that, in this secret, spiritual slumber, He enters more deeply and becomes united to her, not only as formerly, in the faculties that are represented in this verse by the *hills,* but in a much superior degree. He comes *upon the mountains,* that is, the center, and there He touches her truly with His immediate union. She at once perceives that this influence is far different from that in the faculties, and that it is the cause of very great effects, though it is only a transitory touch and not a permanent and lasting union.

Verse 9:

My beloved is like a roe or a young hart: behold, he standeth behind our wall, he looketh forth at the windows, showing himself through the lattice.

While the soul is therefore receiving the sweet caresses of the Bridegroom, she thinks they will last forever; but if they are the pledges of His love, they are also the tokens of His departure. Scarcely has she begun to taste the pleasantness of union before He is wholly gone, and she compares His rapid disappearance to the movements of *a roe or a young hart*.

To comprehend this, let us remember that, between the last trials, which John of the Cross called the "night of the spirit," and the first purification or "night of the senses," God communicates Himself to the soul in a far more perfect manner than He has ever done before. The same thing is indicated here in Song of Songs. The greater the purity and sublimity of this manifestation, the more terrible is the subsequent absence of the Bridegroom and the purification that follows. The measure of His revelation seems to be the measure of His hiding.

These trials are rendered more agonizing because, in addition to the absence of the Divine Spouse, the soul is overwhelmed with a conviction of her own wretchedness, with frightful distress within and persecutions from men and devils without, so that no one can form an idea of her terrible tribulations except from actual experience. The hiding of the Divine Spouse is rightly termed *night* and *death,* for it is He who is the Light and Life of the soul; and as the natural night renders frightful objects far more horrible and terrifying, so the darker the night of the spirit and the less hope there is of beholding another dawn, the more distressing are the accompanying circumstances of the gloom.

While she is fondly lamenting His strange abandonment of her, and when she thinks He is far distant, she suddenly perceives Him close at hand. He had only hidden Himself to try her faith and confidence in Him. However, He never removes His look from her, protecting her more carefully than ever, being more closely united to her than ever before by the new union that has just taken place. But although He always beholds her, she does not always see Him. She only perceives Him occasionally, that she may not be ignorant of His watchfulness, and that she may one day teach it to others. It is to be observed that *he standeth,* since it is now no time to rest, nor even to be seated, but to run; He therefore stands, as if ready to depart.

Verse 10:

My beloved spake, and said unto me, Rise up, my love, my fair one, and come away.

God, having completely turned the soul within and brought her to her center, after having caused her to enjoy His chaste embrace to prepare her for her spiritual marriage, then causes her to take a road that is in all appearances totally the opposite; He brings her out of herself by the mystical death. The Well Beloved, coming in person to address the soul, invites her to go forth from herself in haste. He no longer directs her to take her rest, but commands her to rise up.

This is very different from His former conduct; then He forbade anyone from waking her; now He wants her to rise up at once. He calls her so sweetly and so forcibly that, even if she were not as eagerly bent upon doing His will as she is, she could not resist. *Rise up, my love,* whom I have chosen for My bride, *my fair one,* for I find you lovely, reflecting a thousand traits of My own beauty. Rise up, My dove, simple and faithful, and come forth, for you have all the necessary qualities for leaving yourself. Having led you deeply within, I have come out of you that I may compel you, in following Me, to come forth from yourself also.

This "coming forth" is far different from the one alluded to earlier (see Song of Songs 1:8), and much farther advanced, for the first was only a leaving of natural gratifications, that she might please her Well Beloved. This, however, is a departure from the possession of self, that she may be possessed by God only, and that, perceiving herself no more in self, she may be found in Him alone. It is a transportation of the created being into her Original, as will be shown later.

Verse 11:

For, lo, the winter is past, the rain is over and gone.

There are two winters, one external, the other internal, and these two are reciprocally opposed. When it is winter outside, it is summer inside; in this way, the soul is induced to enter more deeply into herself by an effect of grace, which causes a profound state of contemplation. When it is winter inside, it is summer outside, therefore obliging the soul to come forth from herself by an enlargement produced by a more abundant grace of abandonment. The *winter* of which the Bridegroom speaks in this verse, declaring that it *is past,* is the outward winter, during which the soul might have been frozen by the excessive cold, wet through by the rains, and overwhelmed by the tempests and snows of sins and imperfections, which are so easily contracted in dealings with others. The soul who has found her center becomes so strong that she has nothing further to fear from outside; the *rain* has dried up, and it would be impossible for her, without being guilty of the blackest infidelity, to take pleasure in anything external.

This expression, *the winter is past,* signifies, too, that as winter brings death to everything, so in this soul death has passed over all outward things, so that there is nothing among them that could now satisfy her. If anything should appear to give her pleasure, it only means she has returned to a state of innocence, in which there is no venom as there was before.

Also, the winter *rain is over and gone;* she may go out without fear of the weather and with this additional advantage: that the cold has destroyed what, to her, was formerly alive and would have destroyed her, as the rigor of winter delivers the earth from vermin.

Verse 12:

The flowers appear on the earth; the time of the singing of birds is come, and the voice of the turtle is heard in our land.

To compel her to come forth, He causes her to understand that He is about to lead her into His grounds; He calls them *our land* because He has acquired them for her by His redemption, and they belong to Him for her, and to her through Him. He says that *the flowers* have appeared there, but they are flowers that never fade and no longer fear the coming of winter.

The voice of the turtle, of My humanity, He adds, invites you to lose and hide yourself with it, in the bosom of My Father. That voice will be of greater advantage to you than it is now, when you come into the land to which I call you, which as yet you do not know. This voice of My simplicity and innocence, with which I will satisfy you, is very different from yours.

Verse 13:

The fig tree putteth forth her green figs, and the vines with the tender grape give a good smell. Arise, my love, my fair one, and come away.

There, spring is eternal, and is accompanied, at the same time, without incongruity, by the fruits of autumn and the heats of summer. The Bridegroom points out three distinct seasons; but He no longer refers to winter, for, as has been already stated, when the soul arrives in this new land, she finds that not only the outward, but the inward winter also, is past.

To the soul who has reached God, there is no longer any winter; but there is a season composed of the other three joined in one, which is, as it were, immortalized by the death of winter. For, before reaching the inner winter, the soul has passed through all the seasons of the spiritual life. Afterwards, however, she reenters upon a perpetual spring, summer, and autumn. The mildness of spring does not prevent the fervor of summer nor the fruitfulness of autumn; the heats of summer do not interfere with the beauty of spring nor the abundance of autumn; and the fruits of autumn interpose no obstacle to the enjoyment of spring, nor to the ardor of summer.

O blessed Land! happy are they who are enabled to possess you! We are all entreated, with the spouse, to come out of our selfishness, that we may enter there. It is promised to all, and He who possesses it and to whom it belongs by right of His eternal generation and of the purchase of His blood, earnestly invites us all to proceed there. He furnishes us with all the means of doing so; He draws us by His urgent entreaties. Why do we not hurry?

Verse 14:

O my dove, that art in the clefts of the rock, in the secret places of the stairs, let me see thy countenance, let me hear thy voice; for sweet is thy voice, and thy countenance is comely.

My dove, says the Bridegroom, My pure, chaste, and harmless dove, who are concealed in yourself as in the *secret places,* and who are there hidden in my wounds, which are *the clefts of the* [living] *rock, let me see thy countenance.*

But why do You say this, O Bridegroom? Is not Your beloved wholly turned toward You? Why then do You beg for a sight of her countenance? She is, as it were, wholly hidden in You, and do You not behold her? You want to hear her voice, and she is dumb for everyone else but You!

O admirable invention of Divine Wisdom! The poor soul, thinking that to correspond to her Bridegroom she must continue, as formerly, to contemplate herself and sink still deeper within, endeavors to do so with all her strength; but the contrary is what is required. He calls her outside and wants her to leave herself, and for this reason He says, Let me see thy countenance, *let me hear thy voice;* turn toward Me, for I have moved My place. He assures her that her voice is *sweet,* calm, and tranquil, that in this respect she is like her Beloved, whose voice is not one that is heard by loud speaking. *Thy countenance,* He adds, *is comely.* The superior part of your soul is already fair and has all the advantages of beauty. There is only one thing lacking. Come forth!

If He did not sweetly and forcibly draw the soul outside in this way, she would never leave herself. It would seem that she now finds herself drawn outward with as much force as she formerly felt herself stirred and impelled inward, and even more so, for it requires much more power to draw the soul out of self than to sink it within.

Note here, that before the soul can come forth and abandon self, she must first be led into her own center. She having tasted the enjoyment to be found there, it is difficult to induce her to leave it. But, if she will only be faithful, she will see how infinitely unworthy is the rest in the created center, when compared with that enjoyed in the bosom of the Eternal!

The sweetness she experiences in her savory contemplation is a sufficient inducement, but to leave this enjoyment within, to find nothing but bitterness outside, is a very difficult matter. Besides, by contemplation she lives and possesses herself; but by issuing forth from self, she perishes and dies.

Verse 15:

Take us the foxes, the little foxes, that spoil the vines: for our vines have tender grapes.

The faithful soul asks her Beloved to take away *the little foxes,* which are numerous little defects that begin to appear, for they *spoil* the interior *vines,* which, she says, *have tender grapes.* They are for this reason very delightful to her, and even more so as she expects soon to enjoy the ripe fruit.

How will you be able, poor soul, to abandon these vines to which you are so attached, without being aware of it? Ah! the Master Himself will permit the little foxes to spoil the vines, to destroy the tender grapes, and to make extraordinary havoc with them! Were He not to do this, you would never come forth, because you are so in love with yourself.

Verse 16:

My beloved is mine, and I am his: he feedeth among the lilies.

Oh, inconceivable happiness of a soul wholly and unreservedly devoted to her Beloved, and to whom the Well Beloved is all! The spouse is so enamored of the goodness and caresses of the Bridegroom, manifested for the purpose of obliging her to leave herself, that she thinks she has already arrived at the height of joy and summit of perfection, and that her marriage is now to take place. She says that her Beloved is hers, given to her in whatever measure as pleases Him, and that she is His for the whole extent of His will, that He *feedeth among the lilies* of her purity.

He feeds upon His own graces and virtues, He lives upon innocence and purity, that He may nourish us with the same. He invites us to eat with Him the meat He likes the best, as He gives us to understand by what He says in other verses: "Eat, O friends; drink, yea, drink abundantly, O beloved" (Song 5:1), and, "Hearken diligently unto me, and eat ye that which is good, and let your soul delight itself in fatness" (Isa. 55:2).

Verse 17:

Until the day break, and the shadows flee away, turn, my beloved, and be thou like a roe or a young hart upon the mountains of Bether.

The soul, beginning to be conscious that she no longer perceives the Word, believes that He is only hidden for a night, or rather that He is sleeping in His place of rest. She says to Him, O *my beloved,* since I am under the same roof with You and You are so near me, *turn* a little toward me, that I may perceive You! Let me enjoy the delights of Your companionship until *day break*. In this way, I may have further evidence of Your presence, until the *shadows* of faith *flee away* and yield to the soft light of vision and unclouded enjoyment! Then, remembering the transitory union that she formerly experienced, she cries, Run quickly, if it seems good to You, *like a roe or a young hart* that bounds, but let it be *upon the mountains;* let me once more enjoy that central union that was so sweet and profitable when it was granted to me before.

Chapter 3

Surrendering the Will

*By night on my bed I sought him whom my
soul loveth: I sought him, but I found him
not.*   (Song 3:1)

*T*he soul, finding that the Bridegroom
does not grant her a favor that she
confidently counted on, which He had
formerly bestowed when she did not even hope
for it, is astonished at His prolonged absence.
She seeks Him in her interior, which is her
bed, and during the *night* of faith, but alas! she
is sadly surprised not to find Him! She had
some reason to seek Him there, since it was
there that He had revealed Himself to her and
had given her the most vivid conception of His
character that she has yet experienced. But, O
spouse! You cannot find Him there! Do you not

know that He entreated you not to seek Him any longer in you, but in Himself? You will not now find Him anywhere out of Himself.

Those who have had little experience may object here. They may say that since it is necessary, after all, to come forth out of self in order to seek God in Himself, it would be more reasonable to direct the beginner to seek Him in that way in the first place, instead of sending him the roundabout way of first seeking Him within and then without. But this would be a great mistake. For one who first seeks God in God Himself, looks for Him as for something quite distinct and separate, and, as it were, outside of himself; he even searches heaven for Him. In this way, instead of becoming interior and collecting all the forces of his soul to call upon God, as David did (see Psalm 42), his strength is dissipated and wasted.

We see the slender and scattered lines of a drawing mutually approaching and strengthening each other as they near the central point, but becoming feeble and indistinct in proportion as they recede from there. In the same way, the more the strength of the soul is concentrated in its own center, whether employed with knowing or loving, the more it exhibits a greater power of performing its appropriate work. And as these lines, however widely separated, are united in the focal point, so the functions of the soul, diverse and distinct at a distance from the center, once assembled there, constitute but a single, undivided (though not indivisible) point, and are endowed with a singular power of seeking God.

In order to become interior and spiritual, then, we must begin by seeking God within by contemplation. Without this, we can never reach the central unity. But, when we have once arrived there, we must depart again, not by returning toward the external multiplicity, the point from which we set out, but by passing through and beyond ourselves in order to reach God. For this going forth from self is not effected by the way in which we entered into contemplation. It is effected, as it were, by a way leading through ourselves and beyond: from the center of the created to the center of the Creator.

In short, the center of the soul may be regarded as a sort of inn by which the traveler must necessarily pass, yet in leaving which, he is not obliged to retrace his steps, but may proceed further onward by the high road. And as the way to the inn is longer than the path through which we previously became fragmented and removed from our center, so the further we pass from our center, the further we leave self behind, both in sight and feeling. No sooner do we arrive at our center than we find God, and are invited, as I have said, to come forth from ourselves and to pass onward. And then we indeed pass into Him, for He is truly found where we are no longer. The further we journey, the further we advance in Him, and the further we depart from ourselves.

Then our progress in God should be measured by our separation from self, in relation to our views, feelings, memories, self-interest, and self-reflection. While the soul is advancing toward its center, it is wholly absorbed in self-reflection; and the nearer it approaches, the more intense is its absorption, though in greater simplicity. When, however, it arrives there, it ceases to see itself, just as we see everything around us, but not what is in us. But, to the extent that it moves away from and beyond itself, it sees less and less of itself, in proportion, because its face is turned the other way and it cannot look back. Therefore, those self-reflections, which were useful in the beginning, become exceedingly injurious at the end.

At first, our views must be self-directed and complex. They then become simple and uncomplicated, yet without ceasing to be inclined toward self. And finally the soul is gifted with a single eye. As a traveler who approaches an inn that is in plain sight has no need to deliberate about it, but fixes his eye steadily upon it, and having entered it, no longer beholds it; so the soul, when it has arrived at its center, may be said to behold itself no longer—though, in fact, it has a mode of perception appropriate to its state. When, however, it has passed beyond itself, it no longer feels nor perceives itself. The further it advances in God, the less it discovers itself, until at last, wholly lost in the abyss of God, it no longer feels, knows, nor discerns anything but Him. At that point, it is plain that all self-reflections are hurtful and deadly, for they turn the soul into the path that leads from God, and that would bring it back to self.

Now, this passing beyond self is accomplished through the surrender of the will, which, as sovereign of the faculties, carries with it the understanding and the memory. These, though separate and very diverse powers, are yet one and indivisible in their center. Now, I say, and it is clear, that this state is accompanied by a sort of stability, and the more it advances the firmer it grows. For, it is evident that he who has passed beyond and left self is an entirely different person in his functions from he who is still striving to reach self and his center; and if the former should endeavor to enter the latter road again, he would find it difficult, if not impossible.

So then, we see that those who have reached self and passed beyond it must continuously move a greater distance from it, and those who desire to be converted must continually endeavor to contemplate themselves in their center. To compel a man who has already entered into God, to resume the way and the practices by which he reached his position, would be like endeavoring to force the food that has been digested and passed into the intestines to return by the mouth, a result that only occurs as the sequel to horrible pains and is the forerunner of death. While the food remains in the stomach, however, it may be discharged by vomiting, just as we, while still continuing in self, may return to our ways with greater or less ease, as we are more or less advanced toward the center; but afterward, the thing is far more difficult and almost impossible.

Therefore, depart from self quickly, that you may be no longer except in Him, and there you will find Him! Oh, wonderful plan of the Bridegroom! When He is most enamored of His well beloved, He flies from her with the greatest cruelty; but it is cruelty full of love, and without it the soul would never depart from self, and consequently would never be lost in God.

Verse 2:

I will rise now, and go about the city in the streets, and in the broad ways I will seek him whom my soul loveth: I sought him, but I found him not.

Behold a miracle performed by the absence of God! How many times had He invited His beloved to rise from her repose, and she could not do it? He had entreated her with the most tender expressions, but she was so intoxicated with the peace and tranquility that she enjoyed that she could not be induced to leave them.

O faithful soul! the repose you enjoyed in yourself is but a shadow of that which you will find in God! It had been impossible to rouse her, but now that she no longer finds her Well Beloved in her resting place, she exclaims, Oh, *I will rise now;* this couch that was once paradise to me is now a hell, since my Beloved is gone, and with Him, hell itself would be paradise.

The city, this world that I formerly hated, will be the field of my seeking, she says. The soul is not yet fully instructed, however enamored she may appear and however justly eager she may be for the possession of the Bridegroom, her final end. And therefore she still talks as a child. She is so weak, that she cannot at first seek God in Himself. Although she does not find Him within herself, she must seek Him in everyone she meets, in a thousand places where He is not. And being dispersed in this way, she is occupied with other people under the pretext of seeking the Creator. She seeks, nevertheless, because her heart loves and can find no rest except in the Object of its love; but she finds nothing, because God has not departed from her to be sought in others. He desires to be sought in Himself, and when she arrives there, she will discover another truth, the beauty of which will entrance her: that her Well Beloved is everywhere and in everything, and that everything is He, so that she can distinguish nothing from Him, who is in all places without being enclosed in any.

Verse 3:

The watchmen that go about the city found me: to whom I said, Saw ye him whom my soul loveth?

Since I have not found my Beloved in any mortal creature, she says, I have sought Him among those happy spirits that go about the city to guard it; they *found me* because they are always on the watch. These are *the watchmen* whom God has set upon the walls of Jerusalem, and who will never hold their peace, day or night. (See Isaiah 62:6.) I asked them news of my Well Beloved, of Him for whom I am inflamed with love. But although they themselves possess Him, they could not give Him to me. I think of Mary Magdalene, who, not finding Christ in the sepulcher, seeks Him everywhere, asking angels and men; but none can give tidings of the Beloved but Himself. (See John 20:11–16.)

Verse 4:

It was but a little that I passed from them, but I found him whom my soul loveth: I held him, and would not let him go, until I had brought him into my mother's house, and into the chamber of her that conceived me.

The soul, having therefore come forth from self and having left all others behind, finds her Well Beloved, who manifests Himself to her with new charms. This causes her to believe that the blessed moment for the consummation of the divine marriage is at hand, and that she is about to enter into permanent union. She exclaims in a rapture of joy, *I found him whom my*

soul loveth; I embrace Him and will never let
Him go. For she thinks she can retain Him, and
that He only left her because of some fault she
had committed.

I will embrace Him so closely, she continues, and will attach myself to Him with so
much fidelity, that I will never let Him go until
I have brought Him into *my mother's house,*
that is, into the bosom of God, which is *the
chamber of her that conceived me,* since He is
my Source and Origin.

But what language is this, O foolish soul?
It is His part to take you there, not yours to
lead Him! But love believes that everything is
possible, as Mary was persuaded that she could
carry away the body of the Lord. (See John
20:15.) The soul's intense desire to be there
causes her to forget that she must be there
with Him and clothed with Him, and she says
she will lead Him there.

Verse 5:

*I charge you, O ye daughters of Jerusalem,
by the roes, and by the hinds of the field,
that ye stir not up, nor awake my love, till
[she] please.*

The Bridegroom is full of compassion. After this first trial of the spouse (the first deep,

interior trial since she rose up to come forth),
He again communicates His essential union.
The poor soul is so carried away with the possession of a treasure that seems to her infinitely greater than before—since it has cost
her so dear—that she falls asleep, swoons
away, is lost, and seems as if she is expiring in
the arms of Love.

We may gather from this, that though the
soul suffers greatly in the search for her Beloved, this pain is but a shadow in comparison
with the bliss that arises from the possession
of her adorable Object. The same thing is as-
serted by the apostle Paul, who tells us that
the greatest sufferings of this life are not worthy to be compared with the glory that will be
revealed in us (Rom. 8:18). Her Well Beloved
will not have her awakened because it would
hinder her "death" and delay her happiness.

Verse 6:

*Who is this that cometh out of the wilder-
ness like pillars of smoke, perfumed with
myrrh and frankincense, with all powders
of the merchant?*

The friends of the bride, seeing her
adorned with so many perfections, and so filled
with grace from the visit of the Bridegroom,

testify their astonishment with these words: *Who is this that cometh out of the wilderness like pillars of smoke?*

The bride becomes so purified in the arms of her Beloved, that she issues from them like a subtle vapor, almost consumed by the fire of love. As the result of her uprightness and righteousness, she is like smoke that rises directly upward and is exceedingly subtle. This shows that she is already wholly spiritual. The smoke is composed of the choicest aromas of all the virtues, but it is worthy of mention that the aromas come from gums that melt and powders that are loose and not solid; solidity and consistency are no longer her portion. And where does this upward-tending, aromatic vapor come from? It comes from the wilderness of faith. Where does it go? To its rest in God.

Verse 7:

Behold his bed, which is Solomon's; threescore valiant men are about it, of the valiant of Israel.

The spouse, feeling already quite disengaged from self, thinks that there is only one thing more to be done, and this is true; but alas! what obstacles are yet to be overcome before it is effected. That one thing is to go to

God, who is the *bed* of the True *Solomon*. But
to reach Him, she must pass through *threescore...of the valiant of Israel*. These valiant
warriors are the divine attributes, which are
around the royal bed and prevent the approach
of those who are not in a state of perfect self-
denial. They are the most valiant in Israel, because it is in these attributes that Israel, that
is, the contemplative soul, finds her strength,
and it is also by their means that the power of
God is manifested to men.

Verse 8:

*They all hold swords, being expert in war:
every man hath his sword upon his thigh
because of fear in the night.*

The valiant men of Israel *all hold swords*
to engage in combat with the soul, who, by a
secret presumption, attributes to self what
belongs to God alone. This causes them to exclaim with united voice, "Who is like unto
[God]?" (Exod. 15:11).

The divine righteousness is the first that
comes to fight with and destroy the self-
righteousness of man. And then comes
strength, to bring to nothing the power of
man. By causing the soul to enter, through

the experience of her own infinite weakness, into the strength of the Lord, divine strength teaches her to dismiss all thought except that of the righteousness of God. (See Psalm 71:16.) God's providence attacks human foresight. And so it goes with all the attributes. They are all armed, for it is necessary for the soul to be destroyed in these matters before being admitted to the bed of Solomon, becoming a bride, and reaching the finishing and consummation of her marriage.

Each of these great warriors has *his sword upon his thigh.* This sword is nothing else than the Word of God, deep, searching, and effectual, revealing to the soul her secret presumption, and at the same time destroying it. This is the uncreated Word, who only manifests Himself in the depths of the soul so that there He may act upon what He expresses.

He is no sooner made known than, like a stroke of lightning, He reduces to ashes all who oppose Him. He operated in the same way when He became incarnate. "For he spake, and it was done" (Ps. 33:9), and He engraved upon His humanity the attributes of His omnipotence. He entered into the lowliness of man to bring down man's loftiness, and into man's weakness to destroy his strength; He took the form of a sinner—though He Himself committed no sin—so that He might annihilate self-righteousness. (See Philippians 2:7–8.) He does the same in the soul; He abases, weakens, and covers her with wretchedness.

But why does the Scripture say that the attributes are armed *because of fear in the night?* By this we are to understand that, as self-praise is what keeps the soul in darkness, and is the cause of all her melancholy nights, the divine attributes are armed against it, that it may not usurp that which belongs only to God.

Verse 9:

King Solomon made himself a chariot of the wood of Lebanon.

The Son of God, the King of Glory, *made himself a chariot* of His humanity, to which He became united in the Incarnation, intending to be seated upon it for all eternity and to make of it a triumphal carriage, upon which He will ride with pomp and splendor in the sight of all His creation.

It is made *of the wood of Lebanon,* because He was descended, according to the flesh, from patriarchs, prophets, and kings, eminent for their sanctity and character.[1] The Word of God is in man in the same way, as upon the throne of His majesty, as the apostle Paul declared: "God was in Christ, reconciling the world unto himself" (2 Cor. 5:19).

Christ constructs for Himself in every soul a throne, which He adorns with great magnificence, to become the place of His abode as well as of His repose and eternal delights. He does this after having bought us with His blood and sanctified us by His grace, that He may reign in us as a sovereign. For, as God reigns in Jesus Christ, in the same way Christ reigns in pure hearts, where He finds nothing that either resists or is offensive to Him. In this way, He is appointing us a kingdom and making us

---

[1] Wood of Lebanon: A firmly-rooted, long-lasting cedar tree grown in ancient Lebanon. The wood was durable, did not decay quickly, and was valued as building material. It was also very fragrant. "Cedar played a still-unknown role in the purification rites of Israel (Lev. 14:4; Num. 19:6). Kings used cedar for royal buildings (2 Sam. 5:11; 1 Kings 5:6; 6:9–7:12). Cedar signified royal power and wealth (1 Kings 10:27). Thus the cedar symbolized growth and strength (Ps. 92:12; compare Ezek. 17)." See "Cedar," *Holman Bible Dictionary,* gen. ed. Trent C. Butler, [Nashville, TN: Holman Bible Publishers, 1991].

partakers of His royal state, as His Father had appointed Him a kingdom (Luke 22:29) and shared His glory with Him.

This throne of the King of Kings, then, is made of the wood of Lebanon. The foundation of the spiritual building is the natural ground of man, which is not unsuitably represented by the height and value of the trees of Lebanon, inasmuch as it is derived from God Himself and is made in His image and likeness.

The spouse of the Song of Songs is set forth as a model of this august throne, to every other spouse of the Celestial Bridegroom, that they may become animated in the pursuit of a similar state of happiness. She herself describes the throne, having received new light to examine it with more penetration, in the essential, though transitory, union with which she has just been favored. Therefore, she adds this statement in the following verse:

Verse 10:

He made the pillars thereof of silver, the bottom thereof of gold, the covering of it of purple, the midst thereof being paved with love, for the daughters of Jerusalem.

The *pillars* of the holy humanity of Jesus Christ are made *of silver;* His soul with its powers and His body with its senses are of a finished purity, well represented by the most refined and brilliant silver. The *bottom* stands for Christ's divine nature, in which He exists in the person of the Word. This may be clearly seen in that the surface of this mysterious chariot is made all *of gold,* which, in the Scriptures, often represents God.

The *covering* is adorned with *purple.* What is the significance of this? The bosom of God the Father, which is the dwelling place of the Word, is His by right of His eternal generation. He could have no other dwelling place, even after becoming man by the decree of the Divine Righteousness, to which He voluntarily submitted. Still, He could not reascend to His Father, to enter into the fullness of His glory, except by the purple of His blood. "Ought not Christ to have suffered these things, and to enter into his glory?" (Luke 24:26).

The *midst* of this triumphal carriage is adorned with ornaments of great value, well signified by the word *love* as being the greatest and most precious of all. For is it not Jesus Christ who contains all the treasures of wisdom and knowledge and the fullness of the Godhead bodily (Col. 2:3, 9)? The Holy Spirit was not given by measure to Him (John 3:34). The Holy Spirit, then, fills the midst of this majestic throne, since He is the love of the Father and of the Son, and thus the love with which God loves men; and as He is the union of the divine persons, so He is the link that binds pure souls to Christ. The Divine Solomon has *made* all this for the *daughters of Jerusalem,* who are His elect, for whom He has done and suffered all.

In the sanctuary that God prepares for Himself in His beloved bride, there are, in the same way, *pillars...of silver,* which are the gifts of the Holy Spirit. These are founded upon divine grace, which is like pure and shining silver, and which serves as both material and foundation. The *bottom* is *of gold;* for a soul who is fit to serve as a throne and royal couch for Christ should have no other foundation than God Himself, and must be devoid of every created support. The *covering* is *of purple;* for it is only through much tribulation that we can enter into the kingdom of God (Acts 14:22). And if we must suffer with Christ in order to reign with Him (2 Tim. 2:12), in a much higher degree must this be true of those who are called to the first places in the interior kingdom, and who are to be honored in this life with the nuptials of the heavenly Bridegroom, than it is of the ordinary sort of Christians who leave the world, in a salvable state truly, but loaded with debts and imperfections. The amount of crosses, reproaches, and destruction suffered by such souls is inconceivable. And lastly, the *midst* is *paved with love,* since these living thrones of the Most High, being full of love, are also adorned with all the fruits and ornaments of love, such as good works, merits, the fruit of the Spirit, and the practice of the purest and most solid virtues.

Behold your calling, O daughters of Jerusalem, interior brides, devoted souls! Behold what the King of Kings, the King of Peace, has merited for you and offers to bestow upon you, if you will give Him your love! It is upon this precious foundation that the Bridegroom and the bride rest the magnificent praises that they mutually interchange in the succeeding chapters.

Verse 11:

Go forth, O ye daughters of Zion, and behold king Solomon with the crown wherewith his mother crowned him in the day of his espousals, and in the day of the gladness of his heart.

Christ invites all interior souls, who are the *daughters of Zion,* to go forth out of themselves and their imperfections to *behold king*

Solomon with the crown of glory, bestowed upon Him by God Himself. The divine nature is revealed as a *mother* to mankind: she crowns it, and is at the same time its diadem. She crowns Christ *in the day of his espousals* with a glory as sublime as it is infinite and unfading. But what is the Lamb's espousal day? It is the day on which He ascended into heaven, where He was received at the right hand of the Father, a day of eternal *gladness of heart*. Behold Him, daughters of Zion! arrayed in all His divine conquests, for He desires to share them with you.

Chapter 4

Reflecting His Beauty

*Behold, thou art fair, my love; behold,
thou art fair; thou hast doves' eyes within
thy locks: thy hair is as a flock of goats,
that appear from mount Gilead. (Song 4:1)*

*T*hough the Bridegroom cannot yet admit the spouse to His nuptial bed, which is the bosom of His Father, He nevertheless finds her very *fair,* yes, fairer than ever. For her faults are no longer flagrant sins, nor scarcely offenses. Rather, they are defects in her still hard and contracted nature, which suffers incredible pain in being enlarged so that it may be lost in God. She is then very fair both internally and externally, and fairer than ever, though she cannot be convinced of it because of her recent rebuff from being received into God. Therefore, the Bridegroom assures her that she is very fair, even without that which is concealed from her, and which is more beautiful than anything that may be seen externally, or that can be expressed or imagined.

Your *eyes,* He says, by your fidelity and simplicity, are like those of *doves.* This quality is both exterior and interior. The virtue of simplicity, so highly praised in the Scriptures, causes us to act in the following ways in respect to God: unceasingly, without hesitation; straightforwardly, without reflection; and excellently, without diverse intentions, motives, or designs, with a single eye to the good pleasure of God. When simplicity is perfect, we usually even act without thinking about it. To act in simplicity toward one's neighbor, is to act with frankness, without affectation; with sincerity, without disguise; and with liberty, without constraint. These are the eyes and the heart of the dove that are dear to Christ.

He goes on to say, Your *hair,* which represents the affection that springs from your heart, and which is its ornament, is so separated from earthly things that it is raised above the most excellent gifts until it arrives at

Me. It resembles, in this respect, the *goats* that appear upon the most inaccessible mountains.[1]

Verse 2:

Thy teeth are like a flock of sheep that are even shorn, which came up from the washing; whereof every one bear twins, and none is barren among them.

The *teeth* represent the understanding and memory, which serve to chew and masticate the things we desire to know. These powers, as well as the imagination and the fancy, already have been purified, so that there is no longer any confusion within them. They are appropriately compared to *sheep* that are closely *shorn,* because of the simplicity they have acquired by their union with the Divine Persons.

In this union they have been deprived of their excessive inclination and even of their power to reason and act in a self-reflective and disordered manner, as they formerly did. But though divested of their operations, they are

---

[1] Inaccessible mountains: Mount Gilead, mentioned in the verse, refers to the mountain slopes and tableland northeast of the Dead Sea and east of the Jordan River. The name Gilead means "raw" or "rugged."

not by that process rendered *barren* or unfruitful; on the contrary, they bear double fruit, and that exceedingly pure and perfect, for the powers are never more fruitful than when they are lost with reference to men and are vanished in God their Center.

Verse 3:

Thy lips are like a thread of scarlet, and thy speech is comely: thy temples are like a piece of a pomegranate within thy locks.

The *lips* represent the will, which is the mouth of the soul, because it presses and kisses with affection what it loves. And as the will of this soul loves only her God, and all her affections are toward Him, the Bridegroom compares her to *a thread of scarlet,* which signifies the affections reunited in a single will. This will is all love and charity, since the whole strength of this will is reunited in its Divine Object.

Your *speech,* He adds, is sweet, since your heart has a language that none but I can understand, because it speaks only to Me. *Thy temples are like a piece of a pomegranate,* which has many seeds, all contained in a single rind; in the same way, your thoughts are, as it were, reunited in Me alone by your pure and perfect love; and all that I have thus described is as nothing in comparison with what is yet concealed within your deepest center.

Verse 4:

Thy neck is like the tower of David builded for an armoury, whereon there hang a thousand bucklers, all shields of mighty men.

The *neck* is the strength of the soul; it is a good analogy to compare it with the tower of David, because all the strength of the soul is in God, who is the house of Jesus Christ and of David.[2] For this great king insists, in many places in the Psalms, that God alone is his support, his refuge, his defense, and above all, his strong tower. (See Psalm 18:2; 61:3; 144:2.) The *armoury* is the total abandonment the soul has made of herself to God. Trust, faith, and hope have fortified her in her abandonment; the weaker she is in herself, the stronger she is in God. *A thousand bucklers,* or *shields,* hang upon her Strong Tower to defend her against her innumerable foes, visible and invisible. This is the

---

[2] Tower of David: This was located at the citadel in Jerusalem, which was the palace, or large, fortified home of the king.

armor of such *mighty men* that she fears no attack as long as she remains there, for up to this point, her state is not yet permanently fixed.

— Verse 5:

Thy two breasts are like two young roes that are twins, which feed among the lilies.

The spouse receives facility in helping others, indicated by her *two breasts.* But she does not yet receive this facility in all the fullness that will subsequently be conveyed; it is simply implanted in her as a germ of fruitfulness, the abundance of which is denoted by the *young roes that are twins.* They are twins because they issue from the same Source, Jesus Christ. They *feed among the lilies,* because they are fed on the pure doctrine of Jesus Christ and under His example. This passage is explained more fully in chapter seven, verse three.

Verse 6:

Until the day break, and the shadows flee away, I will get me to the mountain of myrrh, and to the hill of frankincense.

The Bridegroom interrupts His praise of His spouse to invite her to follow Him toward the *mountain* upon which grows *myrrh,* and to the *hill* where *frankincense* is collected. He says, I will go to the mountain of myrrh until the day that the new life you are to receive in my Father begins to appear, and the *shadows,* which envelop you in the obscurity of the most naked faith, *flee away* and vanish. For you will no longer find Me except in bitterness and the cross. It will be, nevertheless, a mountain of exceedingly sweet savor to Me, for the perfume of your sufferings will rise toward Me as incense, and by them I will be enabled to enter into rest within you.

Verse 7:

Thou art all fair, my love; there is no spot in thee.

Until the soul was wholly immersed in bitterness and crosses, though still fair, she was not all fair. However, now that she is prostrate under the load of trouble and affliction, she is *all fair,* and *there is no spot* or deformity in her.

She would now be ready for permanent union if there were not still within her, remains of her former harsh, unyielding, confined, and limited nature, which stands in the way of her happiness. It is not a fault in her, nor is it even offensive in the sight of God; it is simply a natural defect, derived from Adam, which her Bridegroom will imperceptibly take away. But, as for herself, though the cross has entirely destroyed her beauty in the eyes of men, in those of her Bridegroom, she is all fair. Since she no longer has any beauty of her own, she has become possessed of the true beauty.

Verse 8:

Come with me from Lebanon, my spouse, with me from Lebanon: look from the top of Amana, from the top of Shenir and Hermon, from the lions' dens, from the mountains of the leopards.

The Bridegroom calls her by the name of *spouse,* and invites her to hasten in permitting herself to be destroyed and annihilated, and to receive the spiritual marriage. He calls her to her wedding and coronation.

But, O Bridegroom! shall I say it? Why do you so earnestly and so continually invite a spouse to a consummation she so passionately desires? You call her *from Lebanon,* though she is in Jerusalem.[3] Is this because You sometimes

---

[3] Lebanon: This name refers to one or both of the mountain ranges that run parallel to the coast of the Mediterranean Sea. Amana, Shenir, and Hermon, also mentioned in the verse, are part of the eastern range, which is referred to as Anti-Lebanon.

give the name of Lebanon to Jerusalem, or would You perhaps, by the loftiness of this great mountain, indicate the elevation of the spouse in Your eyes? She has hardly a step to take before she will be united to You by an everlasting tie, but when she seems to be approaching Your bed, she is repelled by sixty strong men. (See Song of Songs 3:7.) Is there not cruelty in so powerfully, though sweetly, attracting her toward a treasure that she esteems more highly than a thousand lives, and then, when she seems on the point of obtaining it, roughly repelling her? O God! You invite, You call, You give the fitness for the state before conferring the state itself, as we give a slight taste of a delicious drink that we may excite a desire for more. Ah! what suffering do You not inflict upon this soul by the delay of the gift that You have promised her?

Come...my spouse, He says, for there is but a single step to take before you will have the gift in reality. Until now, I have called you My fair one, My well beloved, My dove, but never, as yet, My spouse. Oh! how sweet is this name! but the reality will be far more pleasant and delightful! Come, He pursues, from the tops of the highest mountains, that is to say, from the purest practice of the most eminent virtues, designated by the mountains of *Amana, Shenir,* and *Hermon,* which are near Mount Lebanon.

However exalted all this may seem to you, and however high it may in fact be, you must come up still higher and surpass everything, so that you may enter with Me into the bosom of My Father and rest there, without any intermediary and by the loss of every means. For immediate and central union can only be accomplished by ascending far above every created thing. But come also from the *lions' dens* and from the *mountains of the leopards,* He says. For you can arrive at a state so divine only by coming through the most cruel persecutions of men and of devils, who are like so many wild beasts. It is now time to rise more than ever above all this, since you are prepared to be crowned as My bride.

Verse 9:

Thou hast ravished my heart, my sister, my spouse; thou hast ravished my heart with one of thine eyes, with one chain of thy neck.

You are *my sister,* since we belong to the same Father. You are *my spouse,* since I have already betrothed you, and there is only a small amount still lacking before our marriage will be consummated. *My sister, my spouse!*

Oh, words of sweetness to a soul in affliction, whose grief overflows because the Beauty she adores, and by whom she is so tenderly loved, cannot yet be possessed!

You have wounded *my heart,* He says, you have wounded My heart! You have inflicted, O spouse, a double wound. The first wound is by *one of thine eyes.* It is as if He were saying, That which has wounded and delighted Me in you, is that all your afflictions, all your humiliations, and your most extreme deprivations have not caused you to turn your eye away from Me in order to behold yourself. You have taken no more notice of the wounds I have caused you to receive, nor even of those that I Myself have inflicted, than if they had not existed. (I have already stated that these wounds are, internally, the apparent desertion of the Bridegroom, which is the most agonizing of the soul's sufferings; and externally, the persecuting malice of men and devils.) For, your pure and upright love kept you so steadily regarding Me, that it did not permit you to consider yourself, nor your own interest, but solely to contemplate Me with love as your Sovereign Object.

But alas! exclaims this afflicted soul, how is it that I have steadfastly regarded You when I do not even know where You are? She does not know that her look has become so purified that, since it is always direct and unreflective, it escapes her notice and she does not perceive that she always sees. And besides, when we can see Him no longer and have forgotten self and every other person, we must of necessity behold God, and the interior eye is fixed upon Him alone.

This fixedness of the interior eye upon God must be unfailingly preserved, though unconsciously; in this way, the spouse never forgets her Bridegroom. Note, too, that the inattention of the spouse to self has its sole origin and cause in her unremitting application of her heart to God. She is therefore free from the mistake of those who put Him out of mind that they may sin without restraint.

The other wound you have inflicted upon Me, continues the Bridegroom, is by *one chain,* or one ringlet of hair, *of thy neck.* This clearly means that every affection of the bride is concentrated in God alone, and that she has lost all her will in His. Thus, the abandonment of her entire self to the will of God, by the loss of all separate will, as well as the integrity with which she clings to God, without any further self-reflection, are the two arrows that have pierced the heart of the Bridegroom.

Verse 10:

*How fair is thy love, my sister, my spouse!
how much better is thy love than wine! and
the smell of thine ointments than all
spices!*

The Bridegroom, foreseeing all the tri-
umphs that the bride will accomplish for Him,
and how abundantly she will nourish innumerable souls, is in an ecstasy of admiration.
For it is to be observed that, the further the
spouse advances, the more love she has, as the
Bridegroom continually replenishes it for her.
Then He cries out, *How fair is thy love, my sister, my spouse!* It is more beauteous than *wine;*
for it provides both wine and milk, one for
strong men and the other for babes.

The smell of thine ointments, by which you
draw souls to Me, infinitely surpasses all
spices. There will be in you an aroma, which
none will recognize except those who are far
advanced, but which will then attract them
and cause them to run after you, that they may
come to Me; and they will be brought to Me by
you. This secret perfume will astonish those
who are ignorant of this mystery. Nevertheless, their experience will compel them to ac-
knowledge: I do not know what it is in you that

attracts me; it is an admirable perfume that I cannot resist, and yet I cannot discern what it is. This must be the ointment of the Holy Spirit, which only the Lord's Christ can communicate to the bride.

Verse 11:

Thy lips, O my spouse, drop as the honeycomb: honey and milk are under thy tongue; and the smell of thy garments is like the smell of Lebanon.

The moment the soul has reached the blessedness of being received forever into her God, she becomes a nursing mother. Fertility is bestowed upon her; she is admitted into the state of the apostolic life, and from that time forward her *lips* continually drip *as the honeycomb,* for the feasting of souls. It is only her lips and not her words, for it is the Bridegroom who speaks through His bride, her lips being yielded to Him as the means of uttering the divine word.

He says, *Honey and milk are under thy tongue,* which I have given you. It is I who place the honey and the milk there, and who cause them to be dispensed for the good of souls, according to their needs. The bride is all honey to those who are to be gained by the sweetness of comforts. She is all milk to those souls who have become perfectly simple and childlike. The scent of your virtues, He says, and of the good works with which you are clothed as with a garment—and which are of no account in your sight, because they are no longer of yourself—is diffused abroad like a sweet smelling perfume.

Verse 12:

A garden enclosed is my sister, my spouse;
a spring shut up, a fountain sealed.

The holy Bridegroom becomes the One who praises the bride, for no other purpose than that He may manifest to us what He wants us to become in following her example.

A garden enclosed is my sister, my spouse, He declares. She is enclosed internally and externally. For as there is nothing within her that is not absolutely Mine, there is nothing outside of her, nor in any of her actions, which is not wholly for Me as well. She is not in control of any of her actions, nor of any other thing whatsoever; she is enclosed on every side; there is no longer anything in her for herself or for any other person. She is also a *fountain,* since she is intimately united to Me, the

Spring from which she derives water to replenish the earth. But I keep her *sealed* so that not a drop will escape without My direction. And, therefore, the water that issues from there will be perfectly pure and without the least mixture, because it issues from Me.

Verse 13:

Thy plants are an orchard of pomegranates, with pleasant fruits; camphire, with spikenard.

Your fertility will be so enlarged that it will be like *an orchard of pomegranates, with pleasant fruits.* United to the Source of all, rendering you useful to all, the Spirit of God will reveal Himself by you in various circumstances, as we see that the pomegranate (which represents souls in the union of love) distributes its sap to every seed that it contains. It is true that the principal sense of this passage concerns the church, but no one would believe the wonderful fruits that a soul who is thoroughly annihilated would produce in behalf of men, as soon as that soul were applied to help them. There are fruits of all sorts in this garden; every soul, in addition to the qualities common to all, possesses characteristics of its own. Thus, one excels in love, the *pomegranate;* another in meekness, the apple; another is distinguished by suffering and the aroma of its good example, the *camphire;* another distills devotion, contemplation, and peace, the *spikenard*. All are assisted by the annihilated spouse, according to their needs.

Verse 14:

Spikenard and saffron; calamus and cinnamon, with all trees of frankincense; myrrh and aloes, with all the chief spices.

The Bridegroom continues His description of the souls, of whom, as the pure result of His goodness, He has made His spouse the mother. And while He is reciting the good qualities of others, He causes them all to be perceived, at the same time, in her, as the channel by which they are distributed.

Verse 15:

A fountain of gardens, a well of living waters, and streams from Lebanon.

This *fountain of gardens* is the Bridegroom Himself, who is the source of the graces that cause spiritual plants to spring up, flourish, grow, and bring forth fruit. The spouse is like *a well of living waters,* and these waters descend from the Bridegroom through the bride, streaming impetuously from the heights of the Divinity, represented by Mount *Lebanon,* to overflow the whole earth. That is, the waters overflow all those souls who sincerely desire to enter into the interior kingdom, and are willing to endure its toils in the hope of enjoying its fruits.

Verse 16:

Awake, O north wind; and come, thou south; blow upon my garden, that the spices thereof may flow out.

The bride invites the Holy Spirit, the Spirit of Life, to come and breathe through her, so that this garden, thus filled with flowers and fruits, may put forth its spicy perfumes for the help of souls. The Bridegroom, too, requires that the resurrection of His spouse be hastened, and that she receive new life by the inbreathing of that life-giving Spirit. The Holy Spirit will reanimate this annihilated soul, so that the marriage may be perfectly consummated.

Chapter 5

The Perfection of the Bridegroom

I am come into my garden, my sister, my spouse: I have gathered my myrrh with my spice; I have eaten my honeycomb with my honey; I have drunk my wine with my milk: eat, O friends; drink, yea, drink abundantly, O beloved. (Song 5:1)

The spouse, as her Well Beloved has declared, is a beautiful garden, always full of flowers and fruits. He comes there to enjoy its delights. It is as though she had said, I desire neither beauty nor fertility except for You. Come, then, into Your garden, and possess all things, partake of and use them for the advantage of favored souls; otherwise, I do not deserve them. The Well Beloved consents to the desire of the spouse. He desires come and partake of everything, but He wants the bride present to see that He Himself first eats from the table He spreads for His friends. *I have gathered,* He says, *my myrrh.* But it is for you, My spouse, for it is your sustenance, which is nothing but bitterness, for suffering never ceases in this mortal life. Nevertheless, this myrrh is never alone, but is always accompanied by very pleasant spices. The perfume is for the Bridegroom; the bitter myrrh, for the spouse. As for Me, says the Bridegroom, *I have eaten my honeycomb...I have drunk my wine with my milk,* I have fed upon the sweets of your love.

Enchanted with the generosity of His bride, He invites all His friends and His children to come and satisfy their hunger and quench their thirst beside His bride, who is a garden laden with fruits and watered with milk and honey. A soul of this strength has abundant supply for the spiritual needs of all sorts of people, and can give excellent advice to all who apply to her.

This is also true of the church that invites Christ to come and *eat,* which simply means to collect the fruit of His merits by the sanctification of His elect, as He will do at His second coming. The Bridegroom replies to His beloved spouse that He did come into His garden when

He became incarnate, that He gathered His myrrh with His spice when He suffered the bitterness of His passion, which was accompanied by infinite merits and sent a perfume up to God the Father.

I have eaten My honeycomb with my honey, He adds. This is to be understood in relation to His actions and His teaching, for He practiced what He preached, and ordained nothing for us that He did not first put in action. In this way, He merited for us, by the very things that He practiced, the grace to do what He requires of us. Thus, the life of Christ was like a honeycomb, the divine order and sweetness of which constituted His meat and drink. They also constituted His happiness, in view of the glory that His Father would receive from it, and the advantage it would be to men.

I have drunk my wine with my milk. What wine is this, O Savior Divine, which You have drunk, and with which You were so deeply intoxicated that You entirely forgot Yourself? It was the overpowering love He bore to men that caused Him to forget that He was God and to think only on their salvation. He was so intoxicated with it that it was said of Him, by a prophet, that He should be loaded with reproaches. (See Psalm 69:9; Romans 15:3.) Such was the strength of His love. He drank wine with His milk when He drank His own blood at the Last Supper, which under the semblance of wine was virgin milk. The milk, again, was the inflow of the divinity of Christ into His humanity.

This Divine Savior invites all His elect to His garden, those who desire to be nourished, like Him, upon suffering, reproaches, and humiliation, and on the love of His example and His pure doctrine. This will be delicious wine and milk for them: wine, which will give them strength and courage to perform everything required of them, and milk, which will delight them by the sweetness of the doctrine that will be taught them.

We are, then, all invited to hear and imitate Jesus Christ.

Verse 2:

I sleep, but my heart waketh: it is the voice of my beloved that knocketh, saying, Open to me, my sister, my love, my dove, my undefiled: for my head is filled with dew, and my locks with the drops of the night.

The soul who watches for its God experiences a state in which, although its exterior appears dead and, as it were, stunned and benumbed like a body in a deep sleep, its heart still constantly retains a hidden vigor that preserves it in union with God. Those souls who are far advanced frequently experience, in addition, a very surprising thing. Often, during the night, they are only half asleep, so to speak, and God seems to operate more powerfully in them in the night and during sleep than during the day.

While asleep, the soul, in this verse, hears clearly the voice of the Well Beloved, who knocks at the door. He desires to make Himself heard; He says, *Open to me, my sister;* I have come to you, *my love,* whom I have chosen above all others to be My bride, *my dove* in simplicity, My perfect one, My beautiful, *my undefiled.* Reflect that *my head is filled* with what I have suffered for you during the darkness of My mortal life, and that for your sake I have been saturated *with the drops of the night,* the most cruel persecutions. I come now to you, to make you a partaker of My reproaches, My ignominy, and My confusion. You have, up to this time, tasted only the bitterness of the Cross; you have not yet experienced its humiliation and confusion. One is quite different from the other, as you are about to learn from a terrible experience.

Therefore, it appears that the whole course of the soul is only a constant succession of crosses, humiliation, and confusion. There are many people who abandon themselves to certain crosses, but not to all, who can never prevail upon themselves to be willing to have their reputations in the sight of men taken away. This is the very point God is aiming at here.

The soul, too, feels an extreme repugnance to obeying the command of God to apply herself outside; she has become fond of her inward retreat. Nevertheless, it is quite certain that she will not have to bear these crosses unless she leaves her solitude. When God intends that a soul shall really die to self, He sometimes permits it to take certain steps that appear false, but are actually true. The result is that its reputation among men is destroyed.

I once knew an interior person to whom a host of most terrible crosses was foreshown, among them the loss of reputation, to which she was exceedingly attached. She could not bring herself to give this up, and begged God to give her any other cross but that, thus formally refusing her consent. She herself told me that she has remained in the same position ever since. So fatal was this reservation to her progress, that she has been favored by our Lord with neither humiliations nor graces since that time.

Verse 3:

*I have put off my coat; how shall I put it
on? I have washed my feet; how shall I defile them?*

The spouse, perceiving the intention of
the Bridegroom to make her a partaker of His
humiliation, is sadly fearful. And she is now as
much dejected at her threatened disgrace, as
she was before bold and courageous in accept-
ing the Cross. There are many who are content
to bear the Cross, but there is scarcely a single
one who is willing to bear its infamy.

The soul is apprehensive, when her possible shame is presented, that she might be rein-
vested with what she has recently thrown aside,
namely, self and her natural defects (defects of
nature, not voluntary transgressions).

In order to purify her spirit, God makes
use of what John of the Cross calls "the obscure night of the spirit," in which He permits
the defects, which the soul thought were vanished and gone forever, to reappear on the surface in very noticeable characteristics. I refer
to natural faults of temperament, hasty words
or actions, impulsive behavior, rebellious
thoughts. As God then strips the soul of her
facility in practicing divine virtues and good

works, all her imperfections reappear and, being abandoned to herself, she suffers on every side. God lays His hand heavily upon her; other people slander her and subject her to the strangest persecutions; her own thoughts are thoughts of rebellion; and the devils besiege her also. It is by this terrible array of crucifying instruments that the soul is made to succumb and yield to death. If any one of them were missing, the part not assaulted in this way would serve the soul as a refuge and a reprieve, and would maintain her in her life of self.

Again, these defects are not voluntary, nor are the thousand wretched weaknesses that assault the soul and make it miserable; but of this the soul is not always conscious, as the absence of God leads her to think that her faults are to blame. Does she turn toward Him? She finds herself cast off and experiences nothing but His indignation. Does she look at self within? She finds only temptations, wretchedness, poverty, imperfection. Does she look imploringly toward others? They are thorns that pierce and repel her. She is suspended, as it were, at a distance from God and every other person. To complete the misery of poor suffering ones like her, He, at such times, commonly thrusts them outside; that is, He makes it necessary, in the order of His providence, for these suffering ones to leave their solitude and mix in the traffic of the world. Their greatest torment is that, while they ardently desire to be wholly detached from others, they find their hearts continually going out after them, in spite of their utmost exertions. But now at last, when others, their own defects, the strength of God's arm, the experience of their own weakness, and the malice of men and devils, have worked out the purposes of God, He delivers them with a single stroke from every foe and receives them perfectly pure into Himself. Those who will not consent to this crucifying process must be content to remain all their lifetime in self and imperfection.

Therefore, in this verse, the spouse purposes to explain that in the beginning the soul suffers persecutions and slander with resolution, from an inward and powerfully sustaining consciousness that they are undeserved, but this is no longer the case. As she finds her thoughts filled with an inclination toward others, she imagines that she has in reality what she really only has in thought. In consequence, she considers herself the most miserable creature in the world, is persuaded that she suffers all her agonies deservedly, and is covered with the most inexpressible confusion and humiliation. She is convinced that there is no one so wicked as herself. The greater her former detachment from others and from spiritual enjoyments and their buoyancy, the more she now feels her wretchedness and her ties to earth and its heavy weight. She experiences all of this in so distressing a degree that she is thrown into agony a thousand times a day. She seems to have an appetite for every pleasure, and to long to enjoy them all, though, in fact, she shuns them more than ever.

The soul is also apprehensive that she might become defiled with human desires. *I have put off my coat,* she says—self, faults, and all the residue of the old Adam that was in me—*how shall I put it on* again? And yet, she continues, I cannot conceive of anything else that can cause my humiliation and confusion. For, regarding the contempt put upon me by others, which is not due to any fault of my own, it is a pleasure and a glory to me, because I trust that it will glorify my God and render me more acceptable in His sight. I ⸱have *washed* and purified my desires, so that there is nothing in me that is not wholly devoted to my Well Beloved; *how shall I* [again] *defile them* by contact with other people?

As I said earlier, at this time the soul is thrust out into active life; that is, her situation or unforeseen circumstance forces her to mingle with the world. She had earlier withdrawn into solitude, painfully separating herself from others, and it is now very distressing to return to them again. Still, if God did not, by His providence, compel her to come forth, she would not be the subject of slander, as she would be unknown. She also would not experience a revival of her desire for others, as they would not be brought before her. She would never be made sufficiently acquainted with her own weakness and her absolute dependence upon grace, or recognize that she can expect nothing from herself, but must wait upon God for everything—must trust in Him, despair of herself, hate her love of self, leaving it forever.

This pain and suffering is not experienced by those who do not know God, nor by those who give themselves up to license. Such people cannot feel the sting of an evil to which they voluntarily subject themselves, quenching the Holy Spirit, giving themselves up to all sorts of deviations, forgetting God, and becoming wickedness itself. The longer they live, the more depraved they become, while the others, after having been tempted, tried, and proven, are deemed worthy—because of their unconscious fidelity and deep humility—of being received into God.

Therefore, the soul says, in this passage, how can I defile my affections? Ah, poor blinded one! what are you trying to ward off? The Bridegroom only desired to test your fidelity and to see if you were truly ready to do all His will. He was despised and rejected of men (Isa. 53:3), esteemed stricken, smitten of God, and afflicted (v. 4), and was numbered with the transgressors (v. 12), He who was innocence itself, and you, who are so loaded with guilt, cannot bear to be reproached with it! Ah! will you not suffer severely for your resistance?

Saint Francis de Sales wrote about this state of the soul:

> The soul cannot remain long in this state of nakedness and plunder, and therefore the apostle [Paul] informs us that after being stripped of the old Adam, we must put on the new man Christ Jesus (Col. 3:9–10). Having renounced and abandoned everything, even our attachment to things good in themselves, and having learned to will neither this nor that, nor anything, but what the Divine Will proposes to us, we must now be clothed again with the same affections. However, we must no longer be clothed with them because they are pleasant, expedient, or fit to gratify our self-love,

but because they are pleasing to God, expedient for His honor, and fit to advance His glory.[1]

Verse 4:

My beloved put in his hand by the hole of the door, and my bowels were moved for him.

The Well Beloved, notwithstanding the resistance of His bride, *puts in his hand* by a little opening that still remains to Him, that is, a remnant of abandonment, in spite of the repugnance of the soul to abandon herself so absolutely. It is important to bear in mind here what was said in the beginning: that there is a voluntary resistance that puts an absolute stop to the work of God, because He cannot violate man's freedom of will, and that there is also a resistance of nature, which lies indeed in the will, but is not voluntary; it is the repugnance of nature to its own destruction. But whatever may be the extent of this repugnance, and however great may be the rebellion of nature against its own annihilation, God does not cease His effectual working to that end. He takes advantage of the consecration the soul has made of herself

---

[1] *Treatise on the Love of God*, Book ix., ch. 16.

and the total abandonment that she has never withdrawn, and does not now withdraw. This is because her will remains submissive and subdued to God, notwithstanding the rebellion in her feelings. It is this abandonment, this submission of the will, which is concealed in the very depths of the soul and is sometimes unrecognized by it, that I have called "the passage of the hand of God," because through it He is able to continue His purifying operations in us without violating our freedom.

The soul in this stage has a depth of submission, to every command of God, that will refuse Him nothing. However, when He unfolds His plans in detail and, using the rights He has acquired over her, calls for the last renunciation and the most extreme sacrifices, then it is that her *bowels* [are] *moved for him,* and she finds trouble where she anticipated none. This difficulty arises from the fact that she has been attached to something without being aware of it. All our troubles spring from our resistance, and these latter instances of resistance come from our attachments; the more we torment ourselves when we are undergoing suffering, the sharper our suffering becomes. But, if we surrender ourselves to our suffering more and more, and permit the crucifying process to go on undisturbed, it is greatly softened. The soul only becomes acquainted with her hindrances as they are removed.

When I spoke earlier of God unfolding His plans in detail, you must not think I mean that He points out to the soul certain things to be renounced and sacrificed; not at all. I have often said that, with God, speaking is doing, and that is the case here. He only explains His plans by putting the soul into the crucible of the most severe trials, as will be seen. He brings her to the point of sacrificing to Him not only her possessions but her entire being, and not only for time but for eternity. And how is this sacrifice accomplished? It is accomplished by an absolute despair of herself, which James of Jesus calls a "holy despair," because it takes away all dependence on man and forces her into an unconditional abandonment of herself into the hands of God. For we must remember that, the more we despair of self, the more we trust in God, though always in a way recognized by the intellect; the further removed we are from certainty and a faith resting on sight, the more deeply we enter into the faith of God, stripped of every foreign support; the more we renounce self, the better we love God.

Whenever God takes anything away from the soul, it is a sacrifice. However, the last sacrifice of all, the one that I am in the habit of describing as the pure sacrifice, is that made by the soul, when, finding herself abandoned by God, self, and man, she cries out to Him, "My God, why hast thou forsaken me?" (Matt. 27:46), and immediately adds, as did the Lord Jesus, "Into thy hands I commend my spirit" (Luke 23:46). This was the entire and absolute sacrifice of Himself, and it is this surrender of the whole of self for time and eternity that I call the last sacrifice; after this, those further words of the Lord Jesus, "It is finished" (John 19:30), announce the completion of the soul's sacrifice, and they close the scene.

All the nature of the soul is in a tremor at the touch of the Bridegroom, for it is painful and causes her the most exquisite anguish. This was what was experienced by the most patient of men, when, after having suffered the most inconceivable ills without complaint, he could not refrain from crying out, when the finger of God was laid upon him, "Have pity upon me, have pity upon me, O ye my friends; for the hand of God hath touched me" (Job 19:21). In the same way, the spouse trembles at the touch of God.

How jealous You are, O Divine Spouse, that your bride should do all your will, since a simple excuse that seemed so just offends You so deeply! Could You not have hindered so dear and so faithful a spouse from offering this resistance?

Note that there are two aspects to her resistance, which relate to the demands made by God in the preceding verses. As we will see, the first has to do with her rebellion against suffering, and the second, against surrendering to the sacrifice of the Cross.

We have heard the voice of the Bridegroom saying to His spouse, "Open to me, my sister, my love!" (Song 5:2), for I am heavy with the drops of My Passion. The soul then sees clearly that He has come to her, loaded with grief, to make her a partaker of His suffering. His words are painful impressions, produced by Himself in her, of all possible grief, attended by all conceivable weakness. For, if she could be strong in her suffering, she would bear it gladly. God opens to her the possibility of loss of reputation and of slanderous persecutions, and follows it up with the reality. He accompanies these troubles with a sense of her own innumerable frailties and wretchedness, an apparent loss of virtue, or rather, of strength and facility for good works, so that she is covered with inconceivable confusion and distress.

For while God lays His own hand heavily upon the interior, He delivers the exterior up to defamation, to the malice of men and often of the Devil, to whom He gives unrestricted power over the body, a thought enough to make one shudder. Ordinarily, before delivering the exterior over to the power of the Enemy, He infuses the soul with such an overwhelming admiration of His justice, and so urgent a desire that its claims should be satisfied, not only in regard to her own sins but to those of others also, that she is almost overcome. Then, the soul, without specification or reserve, and without any viewpoint of her own, surrenders herself to the rigors of divine justice, upon which God takes her at her word. While the trial lasts, she feels an extreme rebellion against the suffering; she can find no trace of abandonment within; she cries with all her strength for deliverance. In the moments of calm that sometimes occur, her appreciation and love of divine justice returns, and she cannot refrain from renewing her sacrifice at the altar of the same justice. Yet, when the tempest resumes, she again forgets her sacrifice and love of justice and, devoured by her repugnance, seems to experience the pangs of death.

At other times, before subjecting the soul to trials, God sets before it, without detail, the most extreme sufferings, and requires its consent. Some souls refuse, not being able to surrender to the sacrifice—some absolutely, others for a few days only. Their resistance causes them horrible torments, especially those who had previously been yielding and obedient, but were unconsciously soiled by a secret pride for their faithfulness in suffering and in never having refused anything to God, however exacting His requirements.

God permits the soul to resist the sacrifice upon the Cross, and to feel this repugnance to receiving a Bridegroom covered with blood and steeped in grief. But souls of this kind seldom resist long. The resistance was necessary to convince them of their frailty and to prove to them how far they are from possessing the courage they foolishly imagined they had.

There are some who, after having had an exquisitely pure experience of the delights of Love, find themselves exceedingly feeble when Love presents His crucifying demands. If they have previously been faithful, the pain of the spiritual impurity incurred by this resistance causes them great suffering.

But, returning to our text, this process is necessary for the soul's perfection. The Bridegroom permits the presence of the fault, so that He may punish and at the same time purge her from the complacency, in her own purity and innocence, that still remains, and from the repugnance that she feels at being stripped of her own righteousness. For, though she knows perfectly well that her righteousness belongs to the Bridegroom, she is still somewhat attached to it, and appropriates some of the credit for it to herself.

Verse 5:

I rose up to open to my beloved; and my hands dropped with myrrh, and my fingers with sweet smelling myrrh, upon the handles of the lock.

No sooner does the soul perceive her fault than she hastens to repent, and to rise up by a renewal of her abandonment and an extension of her sacrifice. This is not done, however, without pain and bitterness. The inferior part and the whole of nature are seized with sadness and terror. Even all her actions are rendered more painful and bitter, but the bitterness is far beyond anything she has yet experienced.

Verse 6:

I opened to my beloved; but my beloved had withdrawn himself, and was gone: my soul failed when he spake: I sought him, but I could not find him; I called him, but he gave me no answer.

It is as though the soul were saying: I have removed the barrier that hindered my total loss and the consummation of my marriage, for that can only take place after total loss. I have therefore removed this barrier by the most courageous abandonment and the purest sacrifice that have ever been seen. I have *opened to my beloved,* thinking that He would come and heal the grief He has caused by His touch.

But alas! the blow would be too mild if the remedy were so promptly applied! He hides, He flies, He has *withdrawn himself,* and is gone. He leaves nothing to His afflicted spouse except the wound He has inflicted, the pain of her fault, and the impurity she believes she has contracted in rising (v. 5).

This opening to her Beloved is a renewed abandonment. Since the resistance she recently exhibited has interrupted her course, the soul must make a new and express act of abandonment. God always demands this, and it shows that the soul has been unfaithful, since she needs to turn again and renew her overt and perceptible acts.

The goodness of the Bridegroom, nevertheless, is so great, that though He hides Himself, He does not cease to bestow great favors upon His friends; and the longer and more severe the privations, the greater the favors. Thus He does to His spouse, who is now in a new and most favorable state of mind, though she does not know it. Her soul had *failed* when He spoke, and by this softening she has lost those hard and unyielding characteristics that have prevented the consummation of the spiritual marriage, so that she is now wholly prepared to flow sweetly into her Original.

Saint Francis de Sales wrote of it in this way:

> David, speaking in the person of our Lord Jesus Christ upon the cross, said, "My heart is like wax; it is melted in the midst of my bowels" (Ps. 22:14). The heart of the Savior, that oriental pearl, precious above all others, and of inestimable value, cast into an unspeakably corrosive sea of bitterness in the day of His Passion, melted within Him, was dissolved, and ran away in anguish under the pressure of such intolerable agonies.
>
> But love is stronger than death (see Song of Songs 8:6), and can touch the heart and soften and melt it more quickly than any other power. "My soul failed when he spake" (Song 5:6), says the holy spouse; and what does she mean to express by this but that her soul was no longer contained within herself, but had flowed toward her Divine Lover. God commanded Moses to speak to the rock, that it should bring forth water (see Numbers 20:8); what wonder, then, if when He Himself speaks softly, the soul of His spouse should melt within her.

Balsam is naturally so thick that it will neither pour nor flow, and the more closely and the longer it is kept, the thicker it becomes, until it is found at last red, hard, and transparent; but by heat it is dissolved and rendered fluid. Love had liquified the Bridegroom, and therefore the spouse called Him an oil poured forth (see Song of Songs 1:3); and now her turn has come, and she proclaims herself as melted with love. My soul, says she, ran down while my Beloved spoke. The love of the Bridegroom was in her heart and under her breasts like new wine, exceedingly strong, which cannot be restrained within its vat, but runs over on every side.[2]

Verse 7:

The watchmen that went about the city found me, they smote me, they wounded me; the keepers of the walls took away my veil from me.

Poor, suffering spouse! Never has anything like this occurred before. For up to this time, the Bridegroom has kept you; you have dwelled securely under His shadow; you were in assurance in His arms. However, since He has departed because of your fault, ah! what

---

[2] *Treatise on the Love of God*, Book vi., ch. 12.

has happened! You thought you had already suffered much by the numerous trials to which He had subjected your fidelity. Yet they were a small matter in comparison with what remains to be suffered. What you have suffered with Him was only the shadow of suffering, and you had no reason to expect any less. Do you think you can espouse a God who was covered with wounds, torn with nails, and despoiled of everything, without being treated in the same way?

The soul finds herself stricken and wounded by those who keep the walls of the city. They who had not before dared to attack her, and who had nevertheless incessantly watched her, now take time to strike her. Who are these *watchmen?* They are the ministers of God's justice; they wound her and take away that covering so dear to her, the *veil* of her own righteousness.

Ah, miserable spouse! what will you now do in your pitiable state? The Bridegroom will have nothing more to do with you after so sad a misfortune, which has subjected you to the humiliation of being maltreated by soldiers, of being *wounded* by them, and even of leaving your veil, your principal ornament, in their hands! If you still continue to seek your Beloved, you will be called mad to present yourself before Him in such a plight. And still, if you do not search for Him, you will die of longing. You are truly in a pitiable condition!

The ministers of God's justice in this verse are devils, to whom He sometimes delivers over souls to be tormented. (See 1 Timothy 1:20.) This happens at times, especially to those who have wavered in their abandonment and have made a resistance to God similar to that of the spouse. This trial, joined to the experience of their own wretchedness, strips them of the support they had in their own righteousness—their own righteousness, remember. That is, it strips them of the claim they had made of the righteousness and fidelity that is manifested in them, as if it were their own.

This appropriation of the things of God to themselves must completely pass away, and all righteousness must be confessed as belonging to Him alone. By the uncertainty in which they are placed regarding their own salvations, through seeing their wretchedness, they are caused to look only to the righteousness of God. They recognize His all and their own nothingness, His omnipotence and their own weakness. And they are therefore established in an abandonment that is never afterwards shaken.

Verse 8:

*I charge you, O daughters of Jerusalem, if
ye find my beloved, that ye tell him, that I
am sick of love.*

True love has no eyes for self. Saint John
Climachus illustrated this when he wrote:

> I have seen three pious men injuri-
> ously treated. The first buried his suffer-
> ings in silence, through fear of the Divine
> Righteousness. The second rejoiced on his
> own account, hoping for the recompense of
> reward, but was afflicted for him who had
> done him wrong. The third, entirely for-
> getful of self, wept at the injury that his
> oppressor had inflicted upon himself by
> wrongdoing. Behold here three worthy
> champions in the lists of virtue! one im-
> pelled by fear, another stimulated by the
> hope of reward, and a third inspired by the
> disinterested breathings of perfect love.[3]

This poor, afflicted spouse forgets her still
bleeding wounds, she forgets her loss, she does

---

[3] *Sacred Ladder,* Degree viii., art. 28. John Climachus (525–605) was Abbot of Mount Sinai in the
Holy Land. His book, also known as *The Ladder of
Paradise,* is a spiritual treatise that illustrates the
monastic life of the time. The work was referred to
as *The Climax of Paradise,* from which John's
name, Climachus, is derived.

not even refer to it. She thinks solely upon Him whom she loves, and she seeks Him with even more perseverance as she finds more obstacles in the way. She calls upon enlightened souls and says to them, O you, to whom my Beloved will no doubt reveal Himself, I charge you by Himself to tell Him *that I am sick of love.*

What, O fairest of women! Do you not want us to tell Him of your wounds, and relate what you have undergone in seeking Him? Ah, no! answers the generous soul, I am abundantly overpaid for my sufferings, since I have borne them for Him, and I prefer them to the greatest good. Say but one word to my Beloved: that I am sick from love! The wound made by His love in the depths of my heart is so acute, that I am insensible to all exterior pains. Yes, I can even say that in comparison they are a delight.

Verse 9:

What is thy beloved more than another beloved, O thou fairest among women? what is thy beloved more than another beloved, that thou dost so charge us?

The daughters of Jerusalem do not cease to call her the *fairest among women,* because her most painful wounds are hidden, and those that are exposed even add luster to her beauty. They are astonished to see a love so strong, so constant, and so faithful in the midst of so many disasters. They inquire, Who is this Well Beloved? For they say, He must be of unequaled attraction, to engage His spouse in this way. For though these souls are spiritual, they are not yet sufficiently advanced to comprehend so narrow and naked a path.

Had the bride thought of herself, she would have said, Call me not fair. (See Ruth 1:20.) She would have used some words of humility, but she is incapable of that. She has only one thought: the search for her Beloved. She can only speak of Him; she can think of nothing else. And though she might see herself plunged into an abyss, it would excite no emotion in her. The reasoning she recently indulged in, through fear of becoming defiled, has cost her too dearly, since it has occasioned the absence of the Bridegroom. Therefore, instructed by her sad experience, she cannot look at herself for a moment; and even if she were as frightful as she is lovely, she could not think of it.

Verse 10:

My beloved is white and ruddy, the chiefest among ten thousand.

My Well Beloved, replies the spouse, is *white* by His purity, innocence, and simplicity. He is *ruddy* by His love, and because He has chosen to be dyed and purpled in His own blood. He is white by His frankness, ruddy by the fire of His love. He is *the chiefest among ten thousand,* that is to say, He is above all. I have chosen and preferred Him to every other. His Father has chosen Him above all the children of men as His beloved Son, in whom He is well pleased (Matt. 3:17). In short, if you want to know, O my young and tender sisters, who it is that I so passionately love, it is He who is fairer than the children of men, for grace is poured into His lips (Ps. 45:2). It is He who is the brightness of the evening, lasting light, the unspotted mirror of the power of God, and the image of His goodness. You judge if I am not right in bestowing upon Him the whole strength of my love!

Verse 11:

His head is as the most fine gold, his locks are bushy, and black as a raven.

The *locks* covering *His head* are to be understood as the holy humanity that covers and conceals His divinity. These same locks, or this humanity extended upon the cross, *are bushy,* like the clusters of the palm. For there, on the cross, dying for men, He achieved His victory over their enemies and obtained for them the fruits of His redemption, which had been promised us through His death. Then the bud of the palm tree opened and the church emerged from the heart of her Bridegroom. There the Humanity, worthy to be adored, appeared *black as a raven,* for He was not only covered with wounds, but also loaded with the sins and blackness of all men, although He was, in truth, unparalleled in whiteness and purity. There Christ appeared "a worm, and no man; a reproach of men, and despised of the people" (Ps. 22:6). Was He not black? And yet this blackness only set off His beauty, for it was only laid upon Him that it might be taken off of the whole world.

Verse 12:

His eyes are as the eyes of doves by the rivers of waters, washed with milk, and fitly set.

She goes on holding up to admiration the perfection of her Bridegroom; His abundance and His wonderful qualities are the joy of the spouse in the midst of her misery. *His eyes,* says she, are so pure, so chaste, and so simple, His knowledge so purified from everything material, that they are like *doves.* They are not like doves of any common beauty, but they are like doves that have been washed in the milk of divine grace. This grace, having been given to Him without measure (see John 3:34), has filled Him with all the treasures of the wisdom and knowledge (Col. 2:3) of God.

He is beside the small streams in lowly souls who, even though they are only a little advanced, are not less agreeable to Him because of their lowliness, especially when they have learned to make use of it. But He makes His constant abode in abandoned souls, near those rapid and overflowing streams that are arrested by nothing in their course, and which swell and rush on with even greater impetuosity when any obstacle seeks to detain them.

Verse 13:

His cheeks are as a bed of spices, as sweet flowers: his lips like lilies, dropping sweet smelling myrrh.

The *cheeks* of the Bridegroom represent the two parts of His soul, the superior and the inferior, which are arranged in such an order that nothing can be conceived of as being more admirable, and which give forth an inconceivable perfume. And as the cheeks are joined to the head, so His noble and beauteous soul is joined to His divinity. The *bed of spices* signifies the powers and interior faculties of His holy humanity, which are all perfectly well-ordered. It was indeed a skillful Perfumer who chose and arranged them, for it was the Holy Spirit who ordered the whole internal and external Man Christ Jesus.

His *lips* are well compared to *lilies,* but they are the exceedingly beautiful red lilies common in Syria. What lips can be more ruby, or fairer, or sweeter, than those that dispense the words of spirit and life, and of the knowledge of eternal life? They also drip with an excellent *myrrh,* for the teaching of Christ leads to repentance, the mortification of the passions, and continual abandonment.

Verse 14:

His hands are as gold rings set with the beryl: his belly is as bright ivory overlaid with sapphires.

His hands are to be understood as His external and internal workings. The interior are all *gold,* for they contemplate nothing less than rendering to God the Father everything received from Him. They are *as rings,* to show that He receives nothing from His Father that

He does not render to Him again, and that He retains nothing. For He is faithful to deliver His kingdom into the hands of His God and Father. (See 1 Corinthians 15:24.) They are *set with beryl,* for every one of His interior operations is distinguished by having the most eminent degree of that virtue to which they belong, especially of devotion to His Father and mercy toward man.

His exterior operations are generous, liberal, and open, in favor of men. Again, His hands are like *rings* because they can retain nothing, and they are full of the most excellent grace and mercy, which He unceasingly communicates and distributes to His needy creation.

His humanity, represented by *his belly,* is compared to *ivory,* because everything in it is exceedingly pure and solid, since all is united to God and rests upon the Divinity. It is adorned and embellished with all possible perfections, which shine in it like so many precious stones.

Verse 15:

His legs are as pillars of marble, set upon sockets of fine gold: his countenance is as Lebanon, excellent as the cedars.

The whole lower part of the body, here spoken of as the *legs* and feet that sustain it, represents the flesh of the Savior; it is well represented by *marble,* because of its incorruptibility. For, although for a few hours it yielded to death, yet, being *set upon sockets of fine gold,* that is, united to the Divinity, it did not see corruption (Acts 2:31); and that noble building of God, sustained by the Word of God, to which it owes its incorruptibility, will never be dissolved.

His countenance is beautiful, even *as Lebanon,* which is of vast extent and is exceedingly fertile, for the cedars are planted there, and they represent the saints. But though all the saints are planted in Jesus Christ, He is nevertheless elect, like them, regarding His humanity, since He is the first fruits of those who are saved. (See 1 Corinthians 15:23.) And He is elected for all men; there is none who is elected who is not chosen in Him and by Him. It is He who has merited their election. They have all been predestined to be conformed to the glory of Christ, that He might be the firstborn among many brothers (Rom. 8:29).

Verse 16:

His mouth is most sweet: yea, he is altogether lovely. This is my beloved, and this is my friend, O daughters of Jerusalem.

The good qualities of ordinary things may be sufficiently well expressed by ordinary words of commendation, but there are some subjects so above expression that they can only be worthily admired by declaring them to be above all praise. Such is the Divine Bridegroom, who, by the excess of His perfections, renders His bride speechless when she endeavors most worthily to praise Him, that all hearts and minds may be attracted to Him. Her passion causes her to burst out in praise of some of the excellencies that seem to her most comely in the Bridegroom. However, as if recovering somewhat from her ecstasy of love, and ashamed of having desired to express what is inexpressible, she condemns herself to sudden silence. In this way, she abruptly ends an address that she uttered as much to find vent for her own passion as to invite her companions to love Him of whom she is so enamored. Her silence is therefore preceded by these few words only, *His mouth is most sweet.*

As the mouth is the channel of the voice, she is signifying that He is the expression of the Divinity, and that therefore, as God, He is superior to all attributes and qualities. If any such qualities are attributed to Him, it is simply an accommodation to the weakness of mankind, which knows no other way of expressing itself. Then, giving herself up to ecstasy, she exclaims, *Yea, he is altogether lovely!*

It is as though she were saying, O my companions! Do not believe me because I have told you of my Well Beloved, but judge for yourselves. Taste for yourselves that He is good (see Psalm 34:8), and then you will understand the force and uprightness of my love.

He is to be desired, too, not only because He is the desire of the everlasting hills and is the desire of all nations (Hag. 2:7), but also because our desire should be to share in His greatness according to our weakness. For He may be imitated by all, though not in all His perfection. This is He, *O daughters of Jerusalem,* who possesses all these rare beauties, and infinitely more than I know how to declare. This is He whom I love and seek, and of whom I am desperately enamored. Judge if I am not justly sick from love.

Chapter 6

Sharing His Divine Nature

Whither is thy beloved gone, O thou fairest among women? whither is thy beloved turned aside? that we may seek him with thee. (Song 6:1)

*T*his soul, in her abandonment and grief, becomes a great missionary; she preaches the perfections, the sweetness, and the infinite loveliness of Him whom she loves, with so much eloquence to her companions, that they are all inspired with a desire to seek Him with her and to know Him themselves. O conquering Love! when You fly away most rudely, then You achieve the most victories! And this soul, impetuous as a torrent by reason of her violent love, carries along with her everyone she meets. Ah! who would not desire to seek and to see so desirable a Lover? O you who are now uselessly throwing away your affections in the amusements of the world, why not join in this search? How infinitely happy would it make you!

Verse 2:

My beloved is gone down into his garden, to the beds of spices, to feed in the gardens, and to gather lilies.

O blessed soul! After your long search, at last you have news of your Beloved! With great confidence you had declared that you would hold Him so firmly that He would never escape, and yet you have let Him go farther off than ever! Alas! she says, I was ignorant and rash. I did not reflect that it was not for me to retain Him; that it is His own prerogative to bestow or withdraw Himself, as seems good to Him; and that I ought to will only His will and to be content with His coming and going. I confess that mine was a selfish love, though I did not know it; I preferred my own pleasure in loving, seeing, and possessing Him, to His good pleasure. Ah! If I could just once see Him again I would do so no longer. I would let Him come and go at His own will, and that would be the way to lose Him no more.

I know, nevertheless, that He has *gone down into his garden.* My Well Beloved is in my soul, but He is so exclusively there for Himself that I desire no part in it. He is in the most interior center, in the most sublime part, where that which is most sweet smelling is found. There is where God dwells, the Source and Seat of every virtue; there He comes to feed on what belongs to Him only, for there is nothing there that belongs to me or is for me. He takes His pleasure in the garden that He has planted, cultivated, and caused to bear fruit by His life-giving heat. Let Him *gather* His *lilies,* then! Let all the purity be for Him! Let Him have all the pleasure and all the profit from it!

Verse 3:

I am my beloved's, and my beloved is mine: he feedeth among the lilies.

The moment the soul is wholly freed from self-praise, she is all ready to be received into the nuptial couch of the Bridegroom. She is no sooner introduced there than, tasting the chaste and holy delights of the kiss of His mouth, which she desired at first (see Song of Songs 1:2*a*), and which she now enjoys in that essential union that has been bestowed upon her, she cannot refrain from expressing her joy in these words: *I am my beloved's, and my beloved is mine!* Oh, wonderful gain! I can describe it no further than that I am unreservedly given up to my Beloved, and that I possess Him without obstacle, hindrance, or restraint!

O, worthy to be envied of the angels! You have at last discovered your Well Beloved, and though you are no longer so bold as to say that you will never let Him go, you have Him more securely than ever. You will never lose Him again! Who would not rejoice with you on so joyful an occasion? You are so fully your Beloved's that nothing hinders you from being lost in Him. Since you have been wholly melted by the heat of His love, you have been ready to be poured into Him as into your final consummation.

Saint Francis de Sales describes it in this way:

> As the Bridegroom had spread abroad His love and His soul in the heart of the bride, so she in turn pours her soul into the heart of her Beloved. As a snowbank upon a hillside exposed to the sun comes forth from itself, gives up its form, and melts and runs away on the side on which

the warmth-giving rays fall upon it, so the soul of the spouse melted and ran toward the voice of her Well Beloved, coming forth from self and the confinement of her nature to follow Him who has called her.

But how is this holy melting of the soul into her Beloved accomplished? The extreme delight of the Bridegroom in the thing loved, produces in her a spiritual impotence, so that she no longer has the power to dwell in self; and thus, like melted balsam, deprived of consistency and solidity, she runs and flows into that which she loves. She does not hurry herself by a sudden effort, nor does she cling and clasp, as though she would become united by force, but she only flows gently along, like a transparent and liquid thing, into the Divinity she adores. And as we see the clouds, thickened and driven by the south wind, melt and turn into rain, and no longer able to contain themselves, fall and run upon the ground, mingling with and tempering the earth so that they become but one with it; so the soul, which, though loving, was still dwelling in self, issues forth in this holy and blessed stream, leaving herself behind forever, not only to be united to her Beloved, but to be wholly mingled and made one with Him.[1]

---

[1] *Treatise on the Love of God*, Book vi., ch. 12.

Ah! exclaims this incomparable spouse, if I am wholly His, He also is wholly mine! For I experience His goodness anew; He bestows Himself upon me in a manner as unspeakable as it is new; He compensates for my pains with the most tender caresses; *he feedeth among the lilies* of my purity. Those lilies of the body are the integrity of the senses. Those lilies of the soul, far more precious to Him than those of the flesh, are an absolute freedom from self-praise. A soul freed from self is a virgin soul.

Verse 4:

Thou art beautiful, O my love, as Tirzah, comely as Jerusalem, terrible as an army with banners.

The Bridegroom, finding His bride entirely free from self, dissolved, and prepared for the consummation of the marriage and to be received into a state of permanent and lasting union with Himself, admires her beauty.[2] He tells her that she is *beautiful* because He finds in her a certain charm and sweetness that approaches the divine. You are as beautiful, He

---

[2] In verse four, the Bridegroom says His bride is as beautiful as Tirzah. Tirzah was a Canaanite city, noted for its beauty. It was one of the cities in the Promised Land that was captured by Joshua.

continues, *as Jerusalem,* for, since you have lost everything of your own to devote it wholly to Me, you are adorned and embellished with all that is Mine and are joint-possessor of all My inheritance. I find you entirely fit to be My dwelling place, as I desire to be yours; you will dwell in Me and I in you. (See John 14:20.)

But while you have so many charms and so much sweetness for Me, you are as *terrible* to the Devil and to sin *as an army with banners;* you put to flight your enemies without a blow, for they fear you as much as they fear Me, since you have become one spirit (1 Cor. 6:17) with God by the loss of yourself in Me.

Ah! poor souls! you who are engaged your whole lifetime in fierce combat and who achieve only insignificant victories, though at the cost of many wounds! if you would only earnestly give yourselves up to God and abandon yourselves to Him, you would be more formidable and more terrible than an infinite army drawn up in battle array!

Saint Francis de Sales wrote this of the soul who is totally yielded to God:

> As the little children of our Heavenly Father, we can walk with Him in two different ways; we may walk in the steps of our own will, conforming it to His and keeping the hand of our obedience always

in that of the Divine Intention, and following wherever that leads. God wills that I should keep holy the day of rest; this binds me to will it too, which I do by an operation of my own will, conforming to the expression of His.

But we may also go with our Lord having no will of our own, simply allowing ourselves to be carried along at His good pleasure, like an infant in the arms of its mother, by a sort of admirable consent that may be called the union, or rather the oneness, of our will with that of God. Such should be our deportment in the manifestation of His good pleasure, as it is developed purely in His providence and without any interference on our part. It is true we may will that all things should happen according to the will of God, and such a will is very good; but we may also receive the manifestations of His good pleasure by perfectly simple tranquility in the will, which, willing nothing, quietly acquiesces in all things that God wills in us, by us, and through us.

Had any one asked the holy child Jesus, as He was held in the arms of His mother, where He went, would He not have been right in answering, I do not go, My mother goes for Me. But, surely, You are going with Your mother? No; I do not go at all, or if I do go where My mother carries Me, I do not go with her nor do I go by My own steps, but by hers. And had anyone replied, But still, O Child beloved! Your will is to allow Yourself to be carried by the dear mother? might He not have answered, Ah no! I have no will about it; as My loving mother walks for Me, so she wills for Me also; I have committed to her the care both of going and of willing to go, wherever she thinks best, and as I walk only by her steps, so I will only by her willing. And as the first suffices for us both, so also does the last, without any willing on My part; I pay no attention to whether she walks fast or slow, this way or that, nor do I concern Myself in the least as to where she goes.

Thus should we be, supple and manageable under the divine good pleasure, plastic as wax, without amusing ourselves with wishing and willing this or that, but committing all things to God that He may will for us as He pleases, casting all our care upon Him for He cares for us (1 Pet. 5:7). Note that the apostle says *all* our care, that is, the care of receiving the events of His providence as well as that of willing or not willing them; for He will see to the well-ordering of our affairs, and will will for us that which is for the best.[3]

---

[3] *Treatise on the Love of God,* Book ix., ch. 14.

Verse 5:

Turn away thine eyes from me, for they have overcome me: thy hair is as a flock of goats that appear from Gilead.

It is impossible to comprehend the delicacy of the love of God, and the extreme purity that He requires of souls who are to be His brides; the perfection of one state is the imperfection of another. Up to this time, the Bridegroom rejoiced infinitely that His spouse never turned her eyes away from Him. Now, He desires her not to look at Him. He tells her, *Turn away thine eyes from me, for they have overcome me.* When once the soul has begun to flow into her God, as a river into its original source, she must be wholly submerged and lost in Him. She must then lose the perceptible vision of God and every bit of distinct knowledge, however small it may be. Remember that we see what is distinct from us, but not what is within us. Sight and knowledge no longer exist where there is neither division nor distinction, but a perfect fusion. The soul in this state cannot look at God without seeing herself, and perceiving at the same time the working of His love. Now the whole of this must be concealed and hidden away from her sight, so that, like the seraphim, she may have her eyes veiled, and may never see anything more in this life. That is, she is not to will to see anything or to make any discoveries of herself, for she cannot do so without infidelity. But this does not hinder God from causing her to discover and understand whatever He pleases. Nothing remains uncovered but the heart, for it is impossible to love too much.

When I speak of distinction, I do not mean the distinction of some divine perfection in God Himself, for that has long since gone. For since the first absorption, the soul has had within her only a single view of God through a confused and general faith, with no distinction of attributes or perfections. And although she has often spoken of the greatness and sovereign qualities of her Well Beloved, this was done only for the purpose of winning souls, and not because she herself had any need for these distinct views, which are given to her according to necessity, either in speaking or writing. The distinction I now refer to is that between God and the soul. Here the soul cannot and ought not any longer to make such a distinction. God is in her and she is in God, since by the consummation of the marriage she is absorbed into God and lost in Him, without power to distinguish or find herself again. The true consummation of the marriage causes a mixture of the soul with God so great and so intimate that she can no longer distinguish and see herself. It is this fusion that diversifies, so to speak, the actions of the one who arrives at this lofty and sublime position, for these actions emanate from a source that is wholly divine, as a result of the unity that has been effected between God and the soul who has been melted and absorbed in Him. God becomes the origin of her actions and words, though they are spoken and manifested externally through her.

The marriage of the body, whereby two persons are rendered one flesh (Gen. 2:24), is only a faint image of this unity by which, in the words of the apostle Paul, God and the soul become one spirit (1 Cor. 6:17). Many are extremely anxious to know when the spiritual marriage takes place; it is easy to ascertain this from what has been said here.

Again, the betrothal, or mutual engagement, is made in the union of the powers when the soul surrenders herself wholly to God, and God gives Himself wholly to the soul, with the intention of admitting her to union; this is an agreement and mutual promise. But ah! what a distance is yet to be traveled, and what sufferings are yet to be undergone, before this eagerly desired union can be granted and consummated! The marriage takes place when the soul falls dead and senseless into the arms of the Bridegroom, who, seeing her more fit for it, receives her into union. But the consummation of the marriage does not come to pass until the soul is so melted, annihilated, and freed from self that she can unreservedly flow into God. Then that admirable fusion of created and Creator is accomplished, which brings them into unity, so to speak, though with the same infinite disproportion that exists between a single drop of water and the ocean. The drop has become ocean; yet, it forever remains a little drop, though it has become assimilated in character with the waters of the ocean, and is therefore fit to be mingled with it and to make but one ocean with it.

If it is said that some saints and some authors have placed the divine marriage in states less advanced than the one that is described here, I reply that it is because they have mistaken the betrothal for the marriage and the marriage for the consummation. In speaking with freedom they do not always distinguish exactly between these degrees, in the same way that the very first steps of the interior road are frequently mistaken for divine union itself. Every soul who has been admitted to the privilege of betrothal considers herself a bride, and very naturally, because the Bridegroom calls her so, as we have seen in this very song. Experience and divine illumination alone can enable someone to distinguish the difference.

Returning to our text, the Bridegroom again compares the thoughts of His spouse, represented by her *hair,* to *goats that appear from Gilead.* He does not compare them to goats that are standing still, for the mind of the spouse is so clear and empty of thoughts, that those that come appear only for a moment and for just so long a time as is necessary to produce the effect God wants to work by them.

Verse 6:

Thy teeth are as a flock of sheep which go up from the washing, whereof every one beareth twins, and there is not one barren among them.

The Bridegroom repeats to His bride what He has already formerly declared, to show her that she now has in full reality what she then had only in the seed. Her *teeth* are her faculties, which have now become so innocent, pure, and cleansed that they are perfectly washed. The *sheep,* which they resemble, are no longer shorn, as they were before. Rather, facility in the use of her faculties, in an admirable manner, and without confusion, is restored. For the memory now only recalls what the occasion demands, according to the Spirit of God, at the right time, and without disconnected images. Her faculties are not barren, since they have been endowed with a double fertility. They are doing more than they have ever accomplished before, and are doing it better.

Verse 7:

As a piece of a pomegranate are thy temples within thy locks.

The rind of the *pomegranate* is the least part of it, and includes all its excellence. It is the same way with this soul. Her exterior appears of small account in comparison with what is concealed within. Her interior is filled with the purest charity and the most advanced graces, but they are hidden under a very common exterior, for God takes pleasure in hiding away the souls He destines for Himself. Men are not worthy to know them, though the angels admire and respect them, even those souls who are hidden underneath the humblest external form in the world. Those who judge by outward appearances alone would believe that

these hidden souls are very ordinary persons,
though they are the delight of God.

Regarding this, John of Saint-Samson
wrote:

> But little can be said of your truly
> abandoned ones who are wholly lost and
> dead to self. No one sees or knows them;
> their dwelling is hidden, and none can tell
> what are their pleasures or the delights in
> which they rest at noon. (See Song of
> Songs 1:7.) Being thus unknown, they are
> often, yes, almost always, persecuted by
> men, even by the best and most holy; in
> this persecution they rejoice and are ex-
> ceeding glad, as it manifests in them the
> life of their beloved Savior. For, since for
> Your love of them You were persecuted by
> Your own children, as bitterly as though
> You had been the enemy of the whole hu-
> man race, is it not a great honor to the
> disciple that he should be as his Master?[4]

He went on to say:

> Holy men even search after persons
> of this degree of abandonment and cannot

---

[4] *Contemplations*, 16. John of Saint-Samson (1571–
1636) was a Carmelite lay brother, mystic, and
writer.

discern them, due to the difference of their states. And thus it comes to pass that they very frequently persecute and outrageously slander, as idle, unknown fellows, those whose lives are profitless, according to their judgment. The fingers of these unknown friends of God, in this way, often distill the choicest myrrh.[5]

These abandoned ones are not they who astonish the world by miracles or the possession of extraordinary gifts; these things are a small matter in their eyes. God hides them for Himself, and is so jealous of them that He will not expose them to the eyes of men. On the contrary, He seals them with His seal, as He Himself declares that His bride is a fountain sealed (Song 4:12), of which He Himself is the seal.

But why does He keep her sealed? Because "love is strong as death; jealousy is cruel as the grave" (Song 8:6). How completely the matter is expressed in this verse, for as death takes away everything from him whom it holds, so Love snatches everything away from the soul and conceals her in the secret recesses of a living sepulcher. The jealousy of God is as cruel as hell, for it will spare no means whatsoever to fully possess the spouse.

---

[5] Ibid., 38.

Truly, O Lord, You are a jealous God! So You call Yourself. (See Exodus 34:14.) One reason for the jealousy of God is the small number of souls who consecrate themselves to Him without reserve. He cannot bear a rival; therefore, He takes only a little delight in divided souls. But He loves and regards as His own special property those who are entirely devoted to Him. He exercises all His rights over them without being interfered with by their freedom of will, since their abandonment is frank, hearty, and perfectly voluntary. However, He is also seized with a jealousy proportionate to His love; He cannot abide a spot in them; they are His choice specimens, locked up in His own secret drawers, and not exposed to the curious gaze of an unappreciative world.

Someone will remind me, perhaps, that the soul cannot be hidden in this manner, since she is a help to her neighbor. But I reply that this is the very thing that most subjects her to humiliation. God makes use of it to render the soul more contemptible because of the contradictions that she must experience. It is true that those who come to her, and are in a state to receive some communication of the grace that is in her, perceive its effects; but besides that, these souls themselves are extremely hidden. God generally permits the humble exterior of the chosen soul to offend even those who are made partakers of her grace, so that they often separate themselves from her after God has produced the effect He intended through her.

In this, the Bridegroom treats the spouse like Himself. Were not all those whom He had gained for His Father offended because of Him? (See Mark 14:27.) Examine for a moment the life of Christ; was there ever anything more ordinary in regard to the exterior? Those who accomplish more extraordinary things are examples of those saints who Christ said would do greater works than He did (John 14:12). The souls of whom we now speak are other Christs, which is the reason we perceive fewer of the features of the saints in them. I refer to those more striking and extraordinary features that sometimes illustrate saints' lives. As to their holiness, that consists simply of the life of Christ in them. But, if we look for the marks of the Lord Jesus, we will find them most clearly in abandoned souls. Nevertheless, He is a stumbling block to the Jews, and foolishness to the Greeks (1 Cor. 1:23). These souls, in their simplicity, frequently offend those who are rather more attached to legalistic methods than to the simplicity of the Gospel, and regard only the rind of the pomegranate without penetrating any further within.

Oh, you who are misled in this way, remember that the pomegranate, to which the spouse is so aptly compared, has a rind very contemptible in appearance, in spite of the fact that it contains the most excellent and agreeable of fruits, both to the eye and to the palate. This is the admirable love that the Bridegroom began to introduce into the heart of His spouse when He first brought her into His store chambers (see Song of Songs 1:4*b*), and which is completed here, the pomegranate now being fully ripened.

Verse 8:

There are threescore queens, and fourscore concubines, and virgins without number.

The Bridegroom declares that there are chosen souls who are like *queens;* there are others of a lower rank, who participate in His special favors, though they do not have the prerogative of sovereigns; and there are great numbers of souls who belong to Him in the ordinary way and who are beginning to sigh for union with Him. However, His bride surpasses them all in the affection He has for her. O God! to what happiness have You raised Your spouse! There are some who appear like queens, elevated above the rest by the splendor of their virtues; there are many others upon

whom You bestow Your caresses; but this Your
spouse is more to You alone than all the others
together.

Verse 9:

*My dove, my undefiled is but one; she is
the only one of her mother, she is the choice
one of her that bare her. The daughters
saw her, and blessed her; yea, the queens
and the concubines, and they praised her.*

Though the primary sense of this verse refers to the universal church, still, as there is
nothing attributed to the church, as a mystical
body, that is not proportionately true of souls as
its members, especially when they are perfectly
pure, so it may be said that there are souls in
every age whom God has chosen in a very special manner. He declares in this verse, then,
that the soul, in whom the marriage has been
consummated by her total annihilation and absolute loss, is a *dove* in simplicity, and *but one*,
for there are few that resemble her. She is also
"but one," because she is restored in God to the
perfect unity of her origin. She is perfect, but
with the perfection of God. And she is perfect
because she has been freed from self and has
been disengaged from her hard, cramped, and
limited nature, ever since the time that, by her

entire renunciation, she entered into the innocence of God. She is perfect in her interior, by the loss of all self-seeking whatsoever.

It is to be noted here that, whatever praises the Bridegroom may have bestowed upon the spouse up to this time, He had never called her *one* and perfect until she had entirely sunk into His divine unity. For these qualities are only to be found in God when the soul is perfected in Him in a permanent and enduring state.

She is *the only one of her mother* because she has lost all the multiplicity of nature and has become separate from everything that is natural. She is the choice one of that Wisdom who bare her, so that she might be lost in His bosom.

The most interior souls have seen her, for God ordinarily permits these souls to be known a little, sometimes bestowing some discernment concerning their state upon other deeply spiritual souls, who are delighted with the sight and, admiring their perfection, pronounce them blessed. The *queens*—souls who are high in the esteem of everyone—and also those other common souls who are inferior in merit, also contribute great praises, because they feel the effect of the grace communicated to them.

Though this may seem to contradict what was said a little earlier, there is, in fact, no inconsistency. What is said here is to be understood in light of the apostolic state of Christ, which He received, as both King and Savior, on the very spot where, a little while afterward, He was executed as a felon.

Verse 10:

Who is she that looketh forth as the morning, fair as the moon, clear as the sun, and terrible as an army with banners?

A chorus of the companions of the Bridegroom are admiring the beauty of His bride. Who is she, they say, who comes forth, rising gradually? For it must be understood that the soul, though in union with God, is raised by degrees and perfected in this divine life until she arrives in the eternal mansions. She rises in God imperceptibly, like daybreak, until she comes to the perfect day and brightness of noon, which is the glory of heaven. But this everlasting day has its beginning in this life. She is *fair as the moon,* for she derives all her beauty from the sun. She is *clear as the sun,* because she is in union with Christ, being a partaker of His glory and lost with Him in God. But she is as *terrible* and fearful to devils, to sin, to the world, and to self-love, *as an army* drawn up in battle array and ready for the fight.

Verse 11:

I went down into the garden of nuts to see the fruits of the valley, and to see whether the vine flourished, and the pomegranates budded.

The soul is not yet so firmly established in God that she cannot still cast some looks upon self; it is an unfaithfulness, but it is rare and only arises from weakness. The Bridegroom has permitted His bride to commit this slight fault in order to show us how much injury is caused by the self-reflection of those in the most advanced states. She entered again for a moment into self under the most false pretexts in the world: to observe the fruits of her annihilation; to see if the vine was flourishing, if she was advancing, if her love had been fruitful. Does that not appear very natural, right, and reasonable?

Verse 12:

Or ever I was aware, my soul made me like the chariots of Amminadib.

I did it, she says, without thought, and not intending to do evil nor to displease my Well Beloved; but no sooner was it done than my soul was in trouble because of *the chariots of Amminadib,* that is, by thousands and thousands of reflections that revolved in my head like so many disastrous chariots. These would have accomplished my destruction if His hand had not sustained me.

Verse 13:

Return, return, O Shulamite; return, return, that we may look upon thee. What will ye see in the Shulamite? As it were the company of two armies.

No matter how advanced the state of the soul may be, if it has departed from God, conviction and conversion are as necessary as at the very first.

The return of the spouse is as ready and sincere as her fault had been slight and unintentional; therefore, her companions did not perceive that she had wandered. The only thing that they observed, and at which they were much astonished, was that scarcely had she finished declaring to them the loveliness and beauty of the Bridegroom than she disappeared from their eyes, because she was then at once admitted to the Marriage Supper of the Lamb. She therefore became so elevated above herself and every other person, that other souls, having entirely lost sight of her, beg her to return to them that they may behold her in her glory and joy as they have seen her in her grief. *Return, O Shulamite!* they cry; temple of peace, *return* to instruct us, both by your example and by your precept, in the way we must take to attain the blessedness that you possess; *return,* that you may be our guide, our support, our consolation; *return,* that you may take us with you.

The Bridegroom replies, in place of His spouse, to those who so earnestly insist that she turn toward them. It is as though He were not pleased that they should interrupt the innocent pleasure she is enjoying in His company, as He had frequently testified to them before by desiring that they not wake her. He says, therefore, Why do you so earnestly beg my bride to return that you may behold her? What will you see in her now that she is one with Me, except, as it were, the *company of two armies* in camp? She has the grace and beauty of a company of young virgins, for the chaste kiss that I have bestowed upon her has infinitely increased her purity. She has, at the same time, the strength and terror of an army, because she is associated with the Holy Trinity and is made partaker of the divine attributes, who are in arms to fight and destroy all the enemies of God in her behalf.

Chapter 7

Bearing Fruit

How beautiful are thy feet with shoes, O prince's daughter! the joints of thy thighs are like jewels, the work of the hands of a cunning workman. (Song 7:1)

O Prince's daughter! O child of God! exclaim the young maidens, your steps are fair both within and without. Those within are very beautiful because she may continually advance in God without any cessation of her rest. It is the enchanting beauty of this advance that it is a genuine rest, which hinders nothing in her progress, and a true progress, which does not in the least interfere with her rest. On the contrary, the greater the rest, the greater the progress; and the swifter the progress, the more tranquil the rest. The external steps are also full of beauty. For she is well ordered, being conducted by the will of God and led in the order of His providence.

How beautiful are thy feet with shoes! Her every step is taken in the will of God, from which she never departs. *The joints of thy thighs* indicate the admirable orderliness of her actions, which take place with an entire subordination of the inferior to the superior part and of the superior to God. He is the *cunning workman* who has melted and shaped this soul in the furnace of love.

Verse 2:

Thy navel is like a round goblet, which wanteth not liquor: thy belly is like an heap of wheat set about with lilies.

The *navel* refers to the capacity of the soul to receive, or to the passive disposition that has been extended and increased to an infinite degree, since she has been received into God. She has not been received solely for her own reception of divine communications, but also that she may conceive and bring forth many children to Jesus Christ. The navel is *round* because it receives much but can contain nothing, receiving only to disperse. The soul is at the same time both fit to receive and prompt in distributing; in this way, she partakes of the qualities of the Bridegroom. She is continually full of *liquor* derived from the fountainhead of the Divinity, and the choicest graces are bestowed upon her for the benefit of others. Her *belly is like an heap of wheat;* for, as wheat sprouts, grows, bears fruit, and feeds the hungry, so her spiritual fertility is abundant in similar excellencies. The belly is surrounded *with lilies* as a sign of the absolute purity of the whole.

Verse 3:

Thy two breasts are like two young roes that are twins.

It would be a small matter for the spouse merely to bear children to the Bridegroom, if He did not also ask her to feed them with His nourishment. The Bridegroom therefore speaks of her *two breasts* to show that she is not only a mother, but a nurse. In truth, not only has she abundant nourishment for her children, but her breasts are always full, though they are incessantly emptied, and there is not an instant when someone is not making some demand upon them. Though they are constantly drawn from in this way, they do not decrease, but on the contrary, their fullness increases with the graces they furnish, so that the measure of their supply is the measure of their fullness. They are very justly compared to *young roes that are twins,* so that we may understand that she derives what she dispenses wholly from God, for, as the young roes depend upon their mother's breast, so the spouse is always attached to Him from whom she receives whatever she communicates to others.

Verse 4:

Thy neck is as a tower of ivory; thine eyes like the fishpools in Heshbon, by the gate of Bathrabbim: thy nose is as the tower of Lebanon which looketh toward Damascus.

The *neck* signifies strength; it is *of ivory* because purity of strength consists in being in God, and for this reason the strength of the spouse is absolutely pure. Her strength is *a tower* where the soul is sheltered from every danger, and from which she discovers the approach of her enemies. Her understanding is referred to as the *eyes,* and when this faculty is lost in God, it becomes a *fishpool,* a source of every blessing and a remedy for every ill. God employs her mind, which has been willingly given up for His sake, in a thousand great undertakings that are useful for the good of her neighbor. The imagination and fancy once disturbed and injured the clearness of her mind, before the spiritual division was effected. But now this is no longer the case, for she is no longer inconvenienced by the frivolous and impertinent intrusion of the senses. God has, as it were, set up a *gate,* or door, between the spirit and the senses.

The *nose* is the symbol of prudence, which has become like *the tower of Lebanon.* It is called a tower because it is strong and impregnable, since it is the very providence and prudence of God, bestowed upon the soul in consideration of her simplicity, by which she has lost all human prudence. This celestial prudence looks only one way; it sees nothing but the divine moment of Providence, and all its foresight consists in receiving what comes from moment to moment. O prudence that is destitute of prudence! how you do surpass the prudence of men, even the most prudent!

Verse 5:

Thine head upon thee is like Carmel, and the hair of thine head like purple; the king is held in the galleries.

The superior part is like a mountain elevated into its God.[1] The *hair,* which represents all the gifts with which the spouse has been favored, belongs so entirely to God that she no longer has any claim upon it. If she has any good or possession, it belongs to the Bridegroom; it is His property. All the adornments and embellishments of the superior part are of royal *purple,* since the soul partakes of the same ornaments with which the King is arrayed.

Verse 6:

How fair and how pleasant art thou, O love, for delights!

God, beholding in His spouse His own perfections, reflected as in a faithful mirror, is enchanted with His own beauty contemplated in her, and exclaims, *How fair and how pleasant art thou* in My beauty, and how glorious is My beauty in you! You are all My delight as I am the delight of My Father. For, representing Me to others, as in a costly mirror, which produces no distortion in the objects held before it, you give Me an infinite pleasure. You are fair and

---

[1] Carmel, mentioned in the verse, is Mount Carmel, a large mountain near the Mediterranean coast of Palestine, west of the Sea of Galilee; it signifies a beautiful, fertile place.

enchanting, for you are clothed with all My perfections. But if you are My delight, I am also yours, and our pleasures are common to both of us.

Verse 7:

This thy stature is like to a palm tree, and thy breasts to clusters of grapes.

Your *stature,* He says, that is, your whole soul, is like *a palm tree,* because of its uprightness. The favors with which I have loaded you have not bent you toward yourself. On the contrary, like a beautiful palm, you are never more erect than when most heavily laden.

The female palm tree has two distinguishing features: one, that the more fruit it bears, the more upright it becomes; and the other, that it will not bear at all except under the shadow of the male. In the same way, this lovely soul has two special qualities: one, that she never inclines in the least toward herself for any grace that she may have received from God; and the other, that she cannot perform the slightest action, however insignificant, by herself, but does all things under the shadow of the Bridegroom, who causes her to do everything in its season. Her *breasts* are beautifully compared to *clusters of grapes.* As the grape, though full of juice, receives none of it for itself, but yields it all to he who compresses it, so this soul, the more she is oppressed and persecuted, becomes more and more benevolent and bountiful to those who do evil toward her.

Verse 8:

I said, I will go up to the palm tree, I will take hold of the boughs thereof: now also thy breasts shall be as clusters of the vine, and the smell of thy nose like apples.

The young virgins, having heard the comparison made by the King of Glory, and carried away with a desire to partake of the graces of the spouse, cry out with one voice; or rather, one, expressing the feelings of the rest, exclaims, *I will go up to the palm tree, I will take hold of the boughs thereof.* I will become a pupil of this mistress of perfection; and if one so wise and so rich will condescend to become a mother to me, I will be her daughter, that I may experience the effects of the anointing of the Bridegroom, which is in her. The fruit of her words will be to me like a cluster of grapes of all exquisite sweetness, and the purity of her teaching will embalm me in its perfume.

Such results follow because God dwells in her. As iron touched by a magnet will attract other pieces of iron, so the soul who is the temple of God attracts other souls by a hidden virtue. People are often brought into a state of prayer and contemplation by simply entering her presence, and they feel more inclination to remain silent than to speak. God then uses this means to communicate Himself to souls; this is a mark of the purity of these unions and affections.

Verse 9:

And the roof of thy mouth like the best wine for my beloved, that goeth down sweetly, causing the lips of those that are asleep to speak.

The young daughter of Zion continues in praise of the spouse. *The roof of thy mouth* refers to the interior of the soul, which is *the best wine,* for it is perfectly fluid and runs into God without being hindered by any obstacle in its own consistency.

It is a wine for God's drinking, for He receives the soul into Himself, changing and transforming her in Him; He makes her His pleasure and delight. He forms and reforms her, causing her more and more to disappear and to be more and more wonderfully transformed in Him. The soul is truly worthy to be the beverage of God, for she alone is capable of making it; and being the beverage of God is also worthy of the soul, since that is her sovereign good and final end.

As Saint Francis de Sales wrote:

> Liquors easily receive whatever shape or boundaries we desire to make them assume, because they have no consistency or solidity in themselves to restrict or interfere with their yielding character. Pour a fluid into a vessel and you will see it rest, quietly bounded by the lines that limit the vase, and assuming perfectly its exact shape. It has no form or figure of its own, but only that of the vessel in which it is contained.
>
> Such, however, is not the natural pliancy of the soul. It has its own set form and sharp outline; the former is due to its habits and inclinations, and the latter to its self-will; and when it refuses to come forth from these, we say that it is hard, that is, obstinate and willful. "I will take the stony heart out of their flesh" (Ezek. 11:19), says the Lord God; that is, I will take away their stiff-neckedness.
>
> Wood, iron, and stone must feel the wedge, the hammer, and the fire before they will change their form; and so must it be with a heart that resembles them in its

hardness and insusceptibility to divine impressions, and remains entrenched in its own will and fortified by the inclinations that follow in the train of our corrupted nature. A heart, on the other hand, that is plastic, soft, and yielding, is called a melted or liquified heart.[2]

Verse 10:

I am my beloved's, and his desire is toward me.

The spouse, being assured of the truth of the assertions of the virgins, confesses and even confirms it. She says, Ever since the ardent love of my Well Beloved has wholly devoured me, I have been so lost in Him that I can no longer find myself. And I can say with a more interior truth than ever before that *I am my beloved's,* since He has changed me into His likeness, so that, as He cannot any longer cast me off, I no longer fear any separation from Him.

O Love! You will no more turn away such a soul as this! And it may be said that she is confirmed in Love forever, since she has been perfected by the same Love and changed into His likeness. The Well Beloved, now seeing nothing in His spouse that is not absolutely of

---

[2] *Treatise on the Love of God,* Book vi., ch. 12.

and for Him, can neither turn away *his desire* nor His looks from her, as He can never cease to behold and love Himself.

Verse 11:

Come, my beloved, let us go forth into the field; let us lodge in the villages.

The spouse can no longer fear anything, since everything has become God for her, and she finds Him equally in all things. She no longer has anything to do with methods nor with being shut up and guarded; she has entered into a glorious participation of the immensity of God. Everything that is said of this inexpressible union is understood with all the essential differences between the Creator and the created, though with a perfect unity of love and of mystical flowing back into God alone. She no longer fears losing Him, since she is not only united to Him, but has been transformed into His likeness. That is why she invites Him to go forth from the enclosure of the house or of the garden. *Come, my beloved,* she says, *let us go* over the world to conquer for You; there is now no place either too small or too large for me, since my place is God Himself, and wherever I am, I am in my God.

Verse 12:

*Let us get up early to the vineyards; let us
see if the vine flourish, whether the tender
grape appear, and the pomegranates bud
forth: there will I give thee my loves.*

She invites her Bridegroom to go everywhere, for she is now full of activity. And, as
God is always acting externally and is constantly at rest within, so this soul, confirmed
within in perfect rest, is also exceedingly active
externally. What she did defectively a while ago,
she now does in perfection. We should note here
that it would have been a serious defect in the
soul if, when she should have remained entirely
passive, she had chosen to act, for in this way
she would have hindered the operations of God;
she would have been acting from her own activity, when God required her to be perfectly passive, that she might die to all self-originated
influences. Now, through her continued passivity, she has become like soft wax, or a perfectly
manageable instrument in the hands of God,
with which He does as He will. She has, then,
reached the only true passivity in its perfection,
an active-passive state, in which her actions are
no longer self-originated, but are wholly due to
the gentle and loving influences of the Holy
Spirit within.

It is no longer herself nor her fruits that she contemplates, but she sees everything in God. In the field of the church she notices a thousand things to be done for the glory of the Bridegroom, and at these she labors with all her strength, according to the occasions presented by Providence, and in the whole extent of her calling.

But, explain yourself, O lovely spouse; what do you mean that you will give your *loves* to your Bridegroom? Is it not He who renders you fruitful and gives you His nourishment? Ah! she means that, being in perfect liberty of spirit and in the enlargement of her soul, since she no longer has any selfish mixture in laboring for His glory, she will give Him the whole fruit of her loves and will cause Him to take in that with which He fills her. He is the Beginning and also the End of her loves, and she desires that they be emptied into Him.

Verse 13:

The mandrakes give a smell, and at our gates are all manner of pleasant fruits, new and old, which I have laid up for thee, O my beloved.

Admirable oneness! All things are common between the Bridegroom and the spouse. As she has nothing that belongs to herself, the possessions of the Bridegroom become common to her also. She no longer has any property or any interests but His, and therefore she says that young and advancing souls, represented by the *mandrakes, give a smell;* it has reached even to us. All that I have, my Well Beloved, is Yours, she says, and all that is Yours is mine. I am so stripped and pillaged of all things, that I have preserved, given, and *laid up for thee all manner of pleasant fruits,* all sorts of excellent actions and results, whatever they may be, without a single exception. I have given You all my works, both the *old,* which You have performed in me from the beginning, and the *new,* which You effect through me from moment to moment. There is nothing that I have not surrendered to You: my soul, with all its powers and operations, and my body, with its senses and everything that it can do. I have consecrated all these things to You, and as You have given them to me to keep, permitting me the use of them, I preserve them wholly for You. I do this so that, regarding both the property and the use of it, all things are yours alone.

Chapter 8

The Final Union

O that thou wert as my brother, that sucked the breasts of my mother! when I should find thee without, I would kiss thee; yea, I should not be despised.

(Song 8:1)

*T*he spouse demands a further sinking into deeper union. Though the transformed soul is in a permanent and enduring union, she is nevertheless like a spouse occupied with the concerns of the household, who must go here and there, though she does not cease to be the spouse. But beyond this, there are moments when the heavenly Bridegroom is pleased to embrace and caress His bride more closely. This is what she now demands. Who will give me, she cries, my Spouse, who is also *my brother,* for we *sucked the breasts* *of my mother,* that is, the Divine Essence? Since He has hidden me with Himself in God, I draw with Him, without ceasing, at the breasts of Divinity. But, in addition to this inconceivable advantage, I desire to find Him alone outside, so that I might enjoy His tender caresses, through which I become more deeply sunk in Him.

John of the Cross gives another equally true and very beautiful turn to this passage:

> When she says, "sucking the breasts of my mother," she means sucking out, drying up, and extinguishing in me the appetites and passions, which are the breasts and milk of our mother, Eve, in the flesh. These are a hindrance in this state. Then, having found You alone without, that is, outside of everything and of myself, in solitude and nakedness of spirit, and, my appetites being destroyed, I may there kiss You in the stillness; and thus my nature, purified of every temporal, natural, or spiritual imperfection, may be made one with all that belongs to You, without the intervention of any other means than love. This is only accomplished in the spiritual marriage, and is the kiss that God receives from the soul. Here no one despises nor dares to assault it, so that it is not annoyed either by the Devil, the flesh, the world, or its appetites,

but that word is fulfilled in it, "The winter is past, the rain is over and gone; the flowers appear on the earth" (Song 2:11–12).[1]

She also asks for another grace that has not been granted until recently: that the outward may be changed and transformed like the inward. For the interior is changed a long time in advance of the exterior, so that, for a considerable time, certain slight weaknesses remain, which serve to conceal the abundance of grace, and do not displease the Bridegroom. They are, nevertheless, a sort of weakness that excites the contempt of man. Let Him so transform my exterior then, cries the spouse, that I will not be despised! What I ask is for the glory of God, and not for my own gain, for I am not able to regard myself any longer.

Verse 2:

I would lead thee, and bring thee into my mother's house, who would instruct me: I would cause thee to drink of spiced wine of the juice of my pomegranate.

The soul, finding herself thus intimately connected with God, experiences two things.

---

[1] *Canticles between the Bridegroom and His Bride,* Stanza 28. (This work is also called *Spiritual Canticle.*)

One is that her Bridegroom is in her as she is in Him. Just as an empty vessel that is thrown into the ocean is full of the same water by which it is surrounded, and contains it without comprehending that within which it is contained, the soul who is borne by her Bridegroom bears Him also. And where does she bear Him? To that place alone where she can go: she bears Him into the bosom of her Father, which is her *mother's house,* that is, the place of her birth.

The other thing that she experiences is that He instructs her there, bestowing upon her the knowledge of His secret things. This knowledge is only given to the favorite spouse, to whom He teaches every truth that is necessary for her to know, or with which, from the excess of His love, He desires her to be acquainted. O wonderful knowledge! communicated with hardly a little stir, in the inexpressible but ever eloquent silence of the Divinity. The Word unceasingly speaks to the soul and instructs her in such a way as to shame the most enlightened teachers.

But, in proportion to what He teaches the soul—communicating Himself to her by degrees, more and more, and continually enlarging her passive capacity—the faithful soul also causes Him to *drink of* [her] *spiced wine* and of the new wine of her *pomegranate*. This is the fruit of love in her, for she perpetually offers up to Him everything that He confers upon her, in the greatest purity. There is a constant flow of intercommunications. The Bridegroom bestows upon the bride and the bride renders to the Bridegroom. O incomparable spouse! shall I say it? You are a partaker of the communion of the Holy Trinity, for you receive without ceasing and give as unceasingly what you receive.

Verse 3:

His left hand should be under my head,
and his right hand should embrace me.

As we have noted before, God has two arms with which •He holds and embraces the spouse. (See Song of Songs 2:6.) One is His omnipotent protection, by which He supports her. The other is the perfect love with which He embraces her, and this holy embrace is nothing else but the enjoyment of Himself and essential union. When the spouse declares that His *hand* should embrace her, she is not speaking of something that has not yet taken place. She is speaking of what has already taken place and what is yet to come to pass.

She received this divine embrace with the nuptial kiss, but she speaks of it as always present and always to come, since it will be continued throughout eternity.

Verse 4:

I charge you, O daughters of Jerusalem, that ye stir not up, nor awake my love, until [she] *please.*

The Bridegroom charges three separate times that His love not be awakened from her sleep, because there are three different sorts of interior slumber. The first is in the union of the powers, in which she enjoys a sleep of a powerful ecstasy, which extends greatly over the senses. At that time, He begs that she may not be awakened because this sleep is then used to detach the senses from the objects that they love impurely; and therefore, the sleep purifies the senses.

The second is the sleep of mystical death, where she expires in the arms of Love. Neither is He willing that she be disturbed in this until she awakens by herself, when the all-powerful voice of God summons her from the tomb of death to the spiritual resurrection.

Of this mystical death in Christ, John of Saint-Samson wrote:

The mystics tell us that there are three characteristics of the dead; they are shrouded, buried, and then trodden underfoot, until the Day of Judgment. It is a striking description of the insensibility of the dead, and we may be confident that we are wholly dead to nature if we discover, by this test, that these requisites exist perfectly in us, and are truly fulfilled in every point. When men shall do with us, whether by the instigation of the Devil or by the permission of God, whatsoever they will, without its causing in us the slightest thought as to its bearing upon ourselves, and this in time as well as in eternity, we may conclude ourselves to be dead as to them. Let us see to it then, whether we are dead or only dying, for the difference between these two states is immeasurable. It is true enough that they who suffer constant agonies are very near to death, but, for all that, they may never wholly die; and it seems to me that it is one of the rarest things in the world to find a man, in these latter times, who is so entirely dead that he may be likened to a corpse in the particulars I have cited above.[2]

Thomas à Kempis also wrote about this state of total abandonment to God:

---

[2] *Spirit of Carmel,* ch. 12.

How rare it is among spiritual persons to find one who is really stripped of everything! Where shall we find the poor in spirit, detached from the love of every creature? We must go to the end of the world before we can find this precious pearl.[3]

The third kind of interior slumber is the slumber of repose in God: permanent, lasting; an ecstatic rest, but sweet, calm, and enduring, and causing no alteration in the senses, the soul having passed into God by her happy deliverance from self. This is a rest from which she will never be disturbed. He does not want His beloved ones to be interfered with in any of their slumbers; He wants them to be permitted to be at rest, for they sleep in His arms.

The first repose is a promised rest, of which pledges are given; the second is a rest bestowed; and the third is a rest confirmed, of which there will be no further interruption. It is not that it could not be broken, for she still has liberty, and the Bridegroom would not say, *until* [she] *please,* if she no longer had the power to will it. However, after a union of this

---

[3] *Imitation of Jesus Christ,* Book ii., ch. 11. Thomas à Kempis (1380–1471) was a Dutch monk and writer.

kind, except if we imagine the most extreme ingratitude and infidelity, she would never do so.

In the meantime, the Divine Bridegroom, while He praises His spouse and permits others to praise her in His presence, desires, at the same time, continually to instruct her. In order to show her that nothing but a vain self-complacency and contempt of others can give rise to so deplorable a result as a departure from Him, He, in the next verse, sets before her the baseness of her origin and the vileness of her nature, so that she may never lose sight of her humility.

Verse 5:

Who is this that cometh up from the wilderness, leaning upon her beloved? I raised thee up under the apple tree: there thy mother brought thee forth: there she brought thee forth that bare thee.

The soul has come up gradually from the desert since she abandoned it (see Song of Songs 3:6), not only the desert of pure faith, but of self. She runs over with delights because she is full; and, like a vessel filled to the brim with water from the spring, she runs over on all sides for the supply of those around her. She no longer supports herself, and therefore she no longer fears the abundance of these delights. She does not fear being overturned, for her Well Beloved, who drops these delights into her bosom, carries them Himself with her, and allows her to walk *leaning upon* Him. O precious gain, the loss of all created supports! God Himself is received for our sole support, in exchange for them!

I raised thee up under the apple tree. I drew you from the sleep of mystical death, raising you from self, from your own corruption, and from the spoiled and corrupted nature that your *mother* gave you by her sin. For, all the operations of God in the soul tend toward two things: one, to deliver it from its actual wickedness and the great evil of its depraved nature; and the other, to restore it to God as fair and as pure as it was before Eve fell under the power of the Seducer. In her innocence, Eve belonged to God without any self-serving inclinations; but she allowed herself to be violated, withdrawing herself from God to commit prostitution with the Devil, and we have all partaken of the evil consequences of that act. We come into the world like illegitimate children who have no idea of their real father, and who cannot be recognized as belonging to God until they are legitimatized by baptism. But even then we still have the traces of that wretched sin. We retain an evil quality that is opposed to God, until He, by long, powerful, and repeated operations, removes it.

In the same way, He draws this soul out of self, depriving her of all its infection, reendowing her with the grace of innocence, and causing her to be lost in Him. He therefore raises her from under the apple tree, an innocent being, raises her from the very place where her mother, human nature, had been corrupted.

Verse 6:

Set me as a seal upon thine heart, as a seal upon thine arm: for love is strong as death; jealousy is cruel as the grave: the coals thereof are coals of fire, which hath a most vehement flame.

The Bridegroom invites the spouse to set Him *as a seal upon* [her] *heart;* for as He is the source of her life, He ought also to be its seal. It is He who hinders her from ever leaving so blessed a state; she is then the fountain sealed (Song 4:12), which none but He can either open or shut. (See Isaiah 22:22; Revelation 3:7.) He desires also that she set Him *as a seal* upon her exterior and her works, so that everything may be reserved for Him and nothing may proceed without His directions. She is then a garden enclosed for her Bridegroom, which He shuts and no man opens, and opens and no man shuts. *For love,* says the Bridegroom, *is strong as death,* to do what He pleases in His beloved. He is as strong as death inasmuch as He causes her to die to everything, that she may live to Him only. But *jealousy is cruel as the grave,* and that is why He encloses His spouse so carefully. So strong is His desire for her utter devotion to Him, that, if we were to imagine that she were to become guilty of the infidelity of withdrawing her abandonment, a supposition as melancholy as it is difficult, she would be instantaneously repulsed from Him into hell by the excess of His indignation. The *coals* are *coals of fire* that enlighten while they burn, and consume while giving light.

O Lamb, who opens and shuts the seven seals (Rev. 5:5), so seal up Your beloved that she may no more go forth except by and for You, for she is Yours by an everlasting marriage.

Verse 7:

Many waters cannot quench love, neither can the floods drown it: if a man would give all the substance of his house for love, it would utterly be contemned.

If the manifold *waters* of afflictions, contradictions, miseries, poverty, and distresses have not been able to *quench* the *love* of this soul, it is not to be supposed that the *floods* of abandonment to the Divine Providence could do it, for it is they that preserve it. Consider a man who has had courage enough to abandon *all the substance of his house* and himself also, that he may possess this pure *love,* which can only be acquired by the loss of all the rest. It is not to be believed that after so noble an effort to acquire a good that he values above all other things, and which is truly worth more than the whole universe, he will afterwards so underrate it that he will return to what he had abandoned. It is not possible. In this verse, God shows us the assuredness and persistence of this state of abandonment to Him, and how difficult it is for a soul who has reached it ever to leave it again.

Verse 8:

We have a little sister, and she hath no breasts: what shall we do for our sister in the day when she shall be spoken for?

The spouse is so happy with her Bridegroom that they have all things in common between them. She speaks with Him of the affairs of other souls, and converses familiarly with Him, as though of their household matters. *What shall we do,* she asks, for this soul, still little and tender, who is *our sister* by reason of her purity and simplicity? (She refers to all like her as if they were one person.) What should be done for her *in the day when* I must begin to communicate with her? For as yet *she hath no breasts,* nor sufficient inclination for the divine marriage; she is not in a condition to assist others; what should we do for her? This is the way in which the spouse should consult with Jesus on behalf of souls.

Verse 9:

If she be a wall, we will build upon her a palace of silver: and if she be a door, we will enclose her with boards of cedar.

The Bridegroom replies, *if* she is already *a wall* of confidence through a well-established passivity, we will begin to *build upon her a palace of silver* for her defense against the enemies of this advanced state, which are human reason, reflection, and the subtlety of self-love. But, if she is as yet but *a door,* just beginning to emerge from multiplicity to enter into simplicity, we will frame her with graces and virtues that will have the beauty and solidity of *cedar*.

Verse 10:

I am a wall, and my breasts like towers: then was I in his eyes as one that found favour.

The spouse, in ecstasies at the instruction and promise that she has just received from the mouth of the Bridegroom, uses herself as an example of the success of this plan. She cries, *I* [myself] *am a wall* of such strength, and *my breasts* [are] *like towers,* which may serve as a shelter and defense to a multitude of souls, and which also keep me assured, since I was *in his eyes as one* [who had] *found favor,* or peace, in God that will never be lost.

Verse 11:

Solomon had a vineyard at Baalhamon; he let out the vineyard unto keepers; every one for the fruit thereof was to bring a thousand pieces of silver.

It seems, O my God, as though You have taken pleasure in forestalling all the doubts and objections that could possibly arise. It might be supposed that this soul, no longer possessing herself and no longer performing any works, no longer has any merit. You, O God, are *Solomon,* who has *a vineyard,* the principal care of which is entrusted to Your spouse, and Your spouse herself is the vineyard. You have rendered Your spouse fruitful and the mother of an innumerable people. You have commissioned Your angels as the *keepers* of the vineyard, and it brings in a great profit both to You, O God, and to the soul herself. You give her the privilege of using and partaking of the fruits; she has the advantage of being scarcely any longer in danger of losing or displeasing You, and, at the same time, of ever ceasing to profit and to merit.

Verse 12:

My vineyard, which is mine, is before me: thou, O Solomon, must have a thousand, and those that keep the fruit thereof two hundred.

The chaste spouse no longer declares as she formerly did, *Mine own vineyard have I not kept* (Song 1:6). It was then a vineyard the charge of which men desired to impose upon her contrary to the will of God. However, as for this one, committed to her as it is by her Bridegroom, ah! what care does she not expend upon it! All things that are ordered in God are in perfect harmony with all kinds of pursuits, whether interior or exterior; and everything is done with wonderful facility, as soon as the person who is charged with it is brought into perfect liberty. The faithfulness of the spouse is worthy of all admiration. For, though she watches with great care her cultivation and guardianship of the vineyard, she nevertheless leaves the whole revenue to the Bridegroom, giving the keepers an equitable salary, but retaining nothing for herself. Perfect love does not know what it is to consider self-interest.

Verse 13:

Thou that dwellest in the gardens, the companions hearken to thy voice: cause me to hear it.

The Bridegroom invites His spouse to speak on His behalf, and truly to enter into the apostolic life by teaching others. He says, You, O My spouse, who *dwellest in the gardens,* in the ever-flowered parterres of the Divinity, where you have not ceased to dwell since winter has passed (see Song of Songs 2:11), you have been in gardens as beautiful for the variety of the flowers with which they are adorned as for the excellence of the fruits that abound in them. You, O My spouse, whom I keep constantly with Me in these gardens of delights, leave, for a moment, the rest full of sweetness and silence that you enjoy there, and *cause me to hear thy voice,* for your *companions* listen.

In these words, the Bridegroom requires of His spouse two things equally admirable. One, that she depart from the profound silence in which she has remained up to this time. During the whole time of faith and her loss in God, she remained in great silence, because it was necessary to reduce her entire being into the simplicity and unity of God alone. Now that she is entirely confirmed in this oneness, He desires to bestow upon her, as a fruit of her completed state, the admirable harmony of multiplicity and unity, in which the multiplicity does not interfere with the unity nor the unity with the multiplicity. He wants her to add to the silent word of the center, which is the state of unity, the outward praise of the mouth.

This is a faint image of what will take place in glory, where, after the soul has been absorbed for ages in an inexpressible silence that is ever eloquent of the Divinity, she will receive her glorified body, which will give perceptible praise to the Lord. Thus, after the resurrection, the body will have its own language of praise, which will add to the happiness of the soul, and not diminish its peace.

Even in this life, when the soul is perfected in a oneness that can no longer be interrupted by external actions, the mouth of the body is endued with a praise appropriate to it, and the beautiful harmony between the silent word of the soul and the perceptible speech of the body constitute the perfection of praise. The soul and the body render praise that is appropriate to what they are; the praise of the mouth alone is not praise; consequently, God says by the prophet, "This people draw near me with their mouth, and with their lips do honour me, but have removed their heart far from me" (Isa. 29:13). The praise that comes purely from the depths of the soul, being silent —and it is more and more silent the more perfect it becomes—is not an absolutely complete adoration, for, since man is composed of soul and body, both should join in giving praise. True perfection in adoration, then, will occur when the body is able to give forth praise of a kind that, far from interrupting the deep and ever eloquent silence of the center of the soul, rather increases it, and when the silence of the soul is no hindrance to the utterance of the body, which will know how to render appropriate worship to its God. Therefore, perfect adoration, both in time and eternity, refers to this resurrection of the exterior word in unity with the interior.

But the soul, accustomed to deep and inexpressible silence, is fearful of interrupting it, and therefore has some difficulty in resuming the exterior word. For this reason, the Bridegroom, to rid her of this imperfection, is obliged to invite her to let her voice be heard. Cause Me to hear your voice, He exclaims. It is time to speak, to speak to Me with your bodily voice, that you may praise Me as you have learned to do during your admirable silence.

In addition to giving her an interior and wholly unspeakable word, God, at times, may endow the soul with the liberty of conversing with Him with great facility, according to His good pleasure. He invites her also to talk to souls about interior things, and to teach them what to do so that they may be agreeable to Him. One of the principal functions of the spouse is to instruct and teach the interior life to the beloved of the Bridegroom who do not have as near an access to Him as does the Shulamite.

This, then, is what the Bridegroom desires of the spouse: that she address Him with both heart and voice, and that she speak to others for Him.

Verse 14:

Make haste, my beloved, and be thou like to a roe or to a young hart upon the mountains of spices.

When the soul, having now no other interest than that of the Bridegroom, either for self or for any other person, and who can will nothing except His glory, sees something that dishonors Him, she cries out, *Make haste, my beloved!* Leave these places that offer You no perfume. Come to those souls who are as *mountains of spices,* who are raised above the rancid vapors that have been corrupted by the wickedness of this world. These mountains owe their sweetness to the scent of the exquisite virtues that You have planted in them, and it is only in such souls that You will find true rest.

The soul, who has arrived at this point, enters so fully into the interests of the Divine Righteousness, both in respect to herself and others, that she can desire no other fate for herself, nor for any other person, than that which the Divine Righteousness would allot—both for time and eternity. She has, at the same time, a more perfect love for her neighbor than ever before, serving him now for God only, and in the will of God. But though she is always ready to be "accursed from Christ for [her] brethren" (see Romans 9:3), like the apostle Paul, and is incessantly laboring for no other end than their salvation, she is nevertheless indifferent regarding her success. She would not be afflicted either at her own damnation or at that of any other person, when regarded from the point of view of God's righteousness. The one thing she cannot bear is that God should be dishonored, because He has set love in order within her; and since then, she has entered into the purest affections of perfect charity.

We must not suppose that the soul who is in the state of this spouse is constantly eager for the conscious presence and sweet and continual enjoyment of the Bridegroom. By no means. She was once in that state of perfection in which she ardently longed for that delightful possession; it was necessary then to attract her on in her progress toward Him, but now it would be an imperfection that she must not entertain.

Her Well Beloved truly possesses her perfectly in her essence and faculties, in a very real and unchangeable manner, above all time and place and means. She no longer has anything to do with sighing for seasons of distinct and conscious enjoyment; and, besides, she is in such an absolute state of abandonment regarding everything, that she could not fasten a desire of any kind upon anything whatsoever, not even upon the delights of paradise. And this state is precisely the evidence that she is possessed at the center. This is why she testifies to the Bridegroom that she is satisfied that He should go where He pleases, visit other hearts, gain them, purify them, and perfect them in all the mountains and hills of the church; that He should take His delight in souls of spices, embalmed in grace and virtue. But, for herself, she has nothing to ask or desire of Him except that He Himself be the author of the emotion. Does she therefore despise or reject the divine visits and consolations? Not at all; she has too much respect and submission for the work of God to do that. But such graces are no longer adapted to her state, annihilated as she is, and established in the enjoyment of the center. Having lost all her will in the will of God, she can no longer will anything. This is beautifully expressed in this verse.

It seems to me very easy to understand that one who places his happiness in God alone, can no longer desire his own happiness. None but he who dwells in God by love can place all his happiness in God alone. And when the soul is disposed in this way, it desires no other happiness than that of God in Himself and for Himself. And, therefore, no enjoyment for selfish ends, not even the glory of heaven, can be a source of satisfaction or, consequently, an object of desire. Desire is always the child of love; if my love is in God alone and for Him alone, without respect to self, my desires will be in Him alone, and will be equally pure of selfish motives.

This desire in God no longer presents the vivacity of the former desire of love, which results from an absence of the thing desired. It has the quietness and repose of a desire completely filled and satisfied. For God is infinitely perfect and forever blessed. And since the happiness of the soul lies in this perfection and blessedness of God, its desires cannot manifest the restlessness of unsatisfied wants, but must present the repose of one who has no ungratified wish. This, then, is the foundation of the soul's state; and this is the reason that it does not perceive in itself all the good desires of those who still love God out of a regard for self, nor of those who love and seek self in the affection that they manifest for God.

It must not be supposed, however, that God cannot implant such dispositions and desires in the soul as may seem good to Him. Therefore,

He sometimes causes it to feel the weight of its tabernacle and to exclaim, "I am in a strait betwixt two, having a desire to depart, and to be with Christ; which is far better" (Phil. 1:23); and, at other times, under the constraining influence of love for others, and of an absolute freedom from every selfish consideration, it will cry out, "I could wish that myself were accursed from Christ for my brethren" (Rom. 9:3).

These apparently contradictory feelings are perfectly reconciled in the depths of souls who never change, so that, though the essential happiness of the soul lies in the blessedness of God in and for Himself, in which all the perceptible desires of the soul are merged and swallowed up, God still excites in it from time to time such desires as seem best to Him. But they are not like those of the former days, which had their basis in the selfish will. They are stirred up and excited by God Himself, without any thought on the part of the soul. He holds it so immovably turned toward Himself, that He is the author of its desires as well as of all its other actions, without any aid from the soul and even without its knowledge—unless He reveals it to the soul directly or through the words that it is led to address to others. A desire that relates to self is the necessary result of a will still contaminated from self. However, as the whole design of God is to destroy the will of a person by making it one with His own, He must, at the same time, necessarily absorb and destroy every self-originated desire.

There is still another reason why God both takes away and implants in the soul, at His own good pleasure, the desires of which it is conscious. Purposing to confer some blessing upon it, He first infuses a desire for the blessing, that He may hear and grant the soul's request. "LORD, thou hast heard the desire of the humble: thou wilt prepare their heart, thou wilt cause thine ear to hear" (Ps. 10:17). He prepares the heart and grants the request. "Delight thyself also in the LORD; and he shall give thee the desires of thine heart" (Ps. 37:4). Since the Spirit makes intercession in and for the soul (Rom. 8:26), its desires and requests are those of the Holy Spirit; and Jesus Christ, dwelling in it, declares, "I knew that thou hearest me always" (John 11:42). An intense desire for death in such a soul would almost certainly be followed by death. The desire for humiliation is far below a desire to enjoy God; yet, since it has pleased God to humble me greatly by means of slander, He has infused into me a great thirst for humiliations. I call it a thirst to distinguish it from desire.

At other times, He inclines the soul to pray for particular things when it is perfectly clear that the prayer has not originated in its own will, but in the will of God. For, it is not free to pray for whom it pleases, nor when it pleases, but when it prays, its requests are always heard and granted. This produces no self-congratulation. The soul is perfectly aware that it is He who possesses it. It is He who prays and grants His own petitions.

Therefore, returning to our text, so great is the indifference of the spouse that she cannot lean either to the side of enjoyment or deprivation. Death and life are equally acceptable; and although her love is incomparably stronger than it ever was before, she cannot, nevertheless, desire paradise, because she remains in the hands of her Bridegroom, as among the things that are not. Such is the effect of the deepest annihilation.

Of this state, Saint Francis de Sales wrote:

> To bless God and to thank Him for every event of His providence is, in truth, a great attainment in holiness. We leave to God alone the care of willing and doing in us, by us, and through us, just what He pleases, without any concern as to what is going on, even though we perceive it distinctly; and if we can, at the same time,

occupy our hearts and fix our attention upon the Divine Gentleness and Goodness, adoring Him with thanksgiving, not in His effects or in the events He ordains, but in Himself and in His own infinite excellence, we will be engaged in a far higher and more blessed employment.

The daughter of a skillful physician lay in a continued fever, and knowing the deep attachment and singular love her father had for her, she said to one of her young friends: I feel a great deal of pain, but the thought of a remedy for it never crosses my mind, for I know nothing of their curative virtues. I might desire one thing when quite another was what I required. Do I not do well, then, to leave the whole care of that matter to my father, who does know, and who can and will do for me whatever is necessary for my recovery? I would do wrong to think about it, for he will think for me; I would do wrong to wish for anything, for he will see that I have everything that is good for me. I will wait, and let him will whatever he thinks best; my only occupation will be to look to him, to testify my filial love to him, and to manifest my implicit confidence in his love.

Her father asked her if she did not desire to be bled, in order to recover? I am yours, my father, she replied; I do not know what I ought to desire in order to get well; you must both will and do for me of your good pleasure (see Philippians 2:13); as for me, it is enough for me to love and honor you with all my heart, as I do.

Behold now her arm bandaged, and her father opening the vein with his lances; but while he cuts and the blood flows, his daughter never turns her eyes from her father's face to behold her bleeding arm, but keeps them fixed upon his countenance with a look of affection, saying nothing, except an occasional expression, My father loves me, and I am wholly his. When all was over, she did not thank him, but only repeated the same expressions of her attachment and filial confidence.[4]

Although the soul, in this state, is more than ever fit to help others, and serves with extreme care those who are sent to her by the Bridegroom, she cannot have a desire to assist others, nor can she even do it, without the special direction of Providence.

For example, the greater the purity and simplicity of a substance, the more extended is its usefulness. Nothing can be purer or simpler than water, and what a vast range of uses it

---

[4] *Treatise on the Love of God,* Book ix., ch. 15.

presents because of its fluidity! Having no perceptible qualities of its own, it is ready to receive all sorts of characteristics with facility; tasteless in itself, it may be infinitely varied in flavor; colorless, it becomes susceptible to every color, in turn. That is the way it is with the spirit and the will in a state of simplicity and purity. Having neither flavor nor color derived from self, God is the author of whatever flavor or color each may manifest, just as the water owes its scent or its hue to the will of him who prepared it. It is not correct, however, to say that the water, however flavored or colored, itself possesses these qualities, inasmuch as they are only incidental and are imprinted upon it from outside; and it is its very quality of freedom from taste and color that enables it to exhibit every variety of both.

Should you ask of this water, What are your properties? it would answer that its property is to have none at all. You may reply, But I have seen you with a red color. It would probably answer, But I am not, for all that, red. I am not so by nature, nor do I reflect upon what is done to me in the impartation of either flavor or color.

It is the same with form as it is with color. As we noted earlier, water is fluid and yielding; it instantly and exactly assumes the form of the vessel in which it is placed. Had it consistency and properties of its own, it could not therefore take every form, receive every taste, exhibit every flavor, and appear with every hue.

I feel that this is the state of my soul; it can no longer distinguish or take knowledge of anything in itself or as belonging to itself, and this constitutes its purity. Instead, it receives everything bestowed upon it, just as it comes, without holding any part of it for itself.